Stephany's Style Secrets

7 Steps to Live and Dress Your Best

By Stephany Greene

STYLE
ICON

Published by Style Icon International
Printed in the United States of America

**STYLE
ICON**

Visit the author's websites: www.stephanygreene.com
                             www.stephanysstylesecrets.com

Cover design by Voodo Fe. Visit www.voodofe.com
Cover photographs by Roy Cox. Visit www.4-optic.com/

Library of Congress PCN Number: #2011906015

ISBN 978-0-615-45331-6

To my parents,
Norma and Bill Byrd,
and Duke Greene...

Thank you for inspiring me to write
ever since I can remember

◆

To my son Tyler

You are the love of my life.
Thank you for loving me for me!

◆

To my fashion students everywhere ...

Go forward and conquer!

ACKNOWLEDGEMENTS

The book you're holding has truly been a labor of love for me. It's filled with advice and guidance I have learned, experienced, been told or observed throughout my life, and especially my career in the fashion business. Seventeen years ago, I had a dream that I wanted to write a book. My dream came true with *Stephany's Style Secrets – 7 Steps to Live and Dress Your Best*. An ocean of people supported and mentored my dream ever since. Several of them were active inspirations for *Stephany's Style Secrets*, some worked with me to design, edit or proofread it, and others were there for me whenever I needed them. In every way, all of the people I want to acknowledge supported my desire to write a book that I am quite proud of, and I thank you, thank you, thank you from the bottom of my humble heart.

To my parents Norma and Bill Byrd, and Duke Greene. Thank you for loving me, educating me and sending me to college, and supporting my undying love for fashion and writing. My son Tyler, I cannot remember what my life was like before you! Your unconditional love and passion bring me joy every minute of every day. My unconditional love for you inspires me to do all of this for you baby, thank you! My brother Brett and my Sister-in-Law Tiffini, thank you for your love and support.

Thank you Rudy "Voodo" Mathalier for designing such a beautiful cover. Your talents never cease to amaze me. Jeannine Silkey, you're the best formatter I know. Dr. Candice A. Pitts, thank you for editing and proofreading in record time. To my Publicist, Lisa White, thank you for your unlimited support and skill at navigating the massive media machine. Gerald Kentopp, thank you for being the best Assistant and friend I could have ever wished for. My mentors Byron Lewis and Ann Ashmore Hudson, I'm grateful for your ultimate wisdom and selfless support. My friends who are more like family, Karen Panish, Nicole Payseur, Michelle Carter, Dr. Jenny Gee, Michelle McGuire, thank you for being there for me through thick and thin. Carl Banks, thank you for believing in me no matter what. Kelita Boyd, Carolene Charles, Dr. Les Vermillion, and David Watts at the University of the District of Columbia (CC), and Scott Bolden, Mariessa Terrell, Peter and Dana Catalano, and Shonika Proctor, thank you for guiding me to the light at the end of my tunnel. My glam squad Gina Marshall, Roy Cox, Gerald Kentopp, and Don Napoleon, you know how to make this chick look and feel fabulous!

Lloyd Boston, Lynda Erkiletian, Oscar Feldenkreis, and Charlene White, thank you for blessing this new journey with your wonderful words of wisdom! You are true visionaries who paved the way for American style to thrive. To my colleagues at the Gap, Bloomingdale's, Essence Magazine, and Nesta Bernard and Natalie Meyers at Howard University, thank you for graciously opening glorious new doors for me to explore. Tommy Hilfiger, designing for you was a dream come true. Thank you for blessing your company with the most culturally diverse environment I ever had the pleasure of working in.

Mere words are not enough to express my gratitude to you all. Thank you, thank you, thank you!!!

Table of Contents

Introduction to Style

I know what you're thinking – how can a book help me dress my best? You've watched every fashion show you can find on TV and have read as many fashion magazines as you can get your hands on. What style secrets can this chick possibly reveal that you haven't heard already?

I'm here to give you THE REAL DEAL. Having great style isn't nearly as difficult as some have led you to believe. I've spent over 20 years as a Fashion Designer and Director for everyone from Calvin Klein to Tommy Hilfiger, Ralph Lauren, Guess, Perry Ellis, the NBA and the NFL, and as a Stylist for a network TV show and various celebrities. A common denominator exists in the worlds of fashion and media that has not been exposed – until now. And I am going to reveal it to you in this book.

The television shows you watch and the books and magazines you read about fashion are fantastic resources and learning tools. And wearing designer clothing may make you feel great – for the moment. However, most TV shows, books, magazines and even designer clothing don't (or can't) tap into the root of why you dress the way you dress. They won't dig deep into the core of your soul to help you figure it out for yourself – with or without them. This is the intangible common denominator I'm talking about. I want to teach you how to be YOU by dressing your best.

I founded the Fashion Merchandising Program at the University of the District of Columbia in Washington, D.C. I am passionate about nurturing and mentoring fashion students. I am especially passionate about them because I know what it's like to walk in their shoes. I know what it's like to sense that 'dressing my best' means far more than the clothes on my back. I know what it's like to have a dream and not know how to reach it. I know what it's like to be stereotyped as the 'creative type' to my face, or an 'airhead', or 'superficial fashionista' behind my back – just because I am in the fashion business. I feel moved to protect and prepare fashion students for the crazy fashion industry they are going to enter. I always knew I could create a great life, but I wasn't always aware of how to do it – without banging my head against a brick wall to get it. It took me years to figure it out. Now that I have, I've written this book for people like you, who are ready to hear real advice because you deserve to create the life you want! Believe it or not, dressing your best can help you do it!

I want to help you learn that your personal power and your personal style are one and the same. When you take steps to unleash your power, you take steps to change your life forever. I took a huge risk to change my life ten years ago. I CHOSE to go from making over $100,000 a year as a fashion designer in New York, to making $3.50 an hour as a waitress in Miami. I didn't do it because I HAD to.

I did it because I wanted – NEEDED – to find happiness in myself, outside of my friends, my love life, my family, my 'things', my career, and especially my stress-filled life that drove me to the emergency room. I had to let go of caring about what other people thought of me in order to be me. I suffered through hearing how 'crazy' some people thought I was. I risked losing friends because I wasn't as cool to them when I was a waitress, as I was when I was designing for people like Tommy Hilfiger (working for Tommy is still one of the best experiences of my life). In the process of finding my happiness, and letting go of unhappy people who weren't the best for me, I simultaneously lost weight that refused to come off before! Go on a bad people diet and watch how fast you lose weight!

The point is, by taking a big risk, I realized...I take myself with me wherever I go. I realized I didn't have to look for happiness outside myself. It was never in my designer clothes, my seemingly glamorous career, my man, or even my friends. Happiness existed in me all along. I just had to discover it. And, for a while, I was actually happier making $3.50 an hour as a waitress than I ever was as an overly stressed out fashion executive making $100,000 a year because I had found peace in being me.

My life is the fuel I've used to become successful, to become powerful, and to become, dare I say it, stylish. You can too. I've developed seven style secrets that will allow you to unleash your power to step into a life that is stunning. From this moment forward, you can have the happiness you deserve, a look that is entirely you, and the courage to dare to do MORE. There are **no more limits** to your power! There are **no more obstacles** in your way!

What will this look like in your life? I don't want to spoil the end of the story, but a powerful woman gets what she wants. You can get that job you've always wanted. You can find a partner who truly loves you for you. You can see your dreams fully realized. All it takes is power – and I want you to snatch it back from anything or anyone who ever stole it from you.

You'll notice that I purposefully chose not to use any pictures in this book. You don't need pictures from me. You are inundated by thousands of images on TV, websites and billboards, in books, advertisements and magazines that tell you how you 'should' look…every day…all the time. Instead, look inside yourself while you join me on this journey of discovering what is best for you.

You're holding the book that will enable you to break down all the barriers that prevented you from 'designing' the life you deserve. Today is the day you can start to empower yourself to find your own personal style, and more importantly, your own personal power. You have powers right now that are just waiting to be unleashed into the world. What exists deep inside you that you're dying to share?

Stephany's Style Secrets will do more than teach the *7 Steps to Live and Dress Your Best*. It will teach you how to dress your best and live your best life for the rest of your life.

1

Why Are You Here?

This is not your average fluffy fashion book. Hold on to your hat honey because you're in for a wild ride. Let's keep it real. For one reason or another, you're not happy. I want to make you happy. By the time you finish this book, I hope you will be.

When you walk into a room, your brain doesn't make an entrance.

You do.

It's not your personality that turns heads.

It's the way you look.

It's a fact – your appearance makes an instant impression, no matter what you think.

Most people are more focused on what you wear, than who you are. The labels on your clothing used to be the most important part of your outfit. Then came the size of your outfit. The closer you got to zero, the better you looked and the more fashionable you were.

Well, that's still the case, isn't it?

Not in my book!

It's time to redefine what fashion is. Instead of looking at fashion as an article of clothing, it's time to look at how fashion is a verb.

Fashion is something you DO, not just something you wear.

Style is something that you DO, not just something you wear.

You can use the clothing you wear to become anyone, to feel anything, and to unleash the parts of you that no one knows until they talk to you.

FASHION: (v.) to give a particular shape or form to; make: to accommodate; adjust; adapt (*Webster's Dictionary*)

STYLE: (v.) to do decorative work with a style; to design or arrange in accordance with a given or new style: to style an evening dress; to style one's hair; to bring into conformity with a specific style or give a specific style to (*Webster's Dictionary*)

As you can see, these words aren't things (or nouns) and they certainly aren't static.

To me, style is an evolution about movement,--moving from who you are right now to who you could be, to who you truly are.

At the core of fashion and at the core of style is truth. When you are true to yourself and the way you feel about yourself, you will begin to express this part of yourself in the way you dress, the way you act, and the way you live in the world.

To become fashionable isn't about becoming society's version of what "they" think you *should* look like.

To become fashionable, to uncover your style is to uncover something much more special, something much more unique.

To find your style is to find yourself.

And you are beautiful.

Why Now?

You're here because there is a disconnection between how you feel and how you want to feel. You and your self esteem haven't been introduced to each other in a while.

What you want and who you are don't have to be estranged anymore. You can connect these parts of yourself together. You can reconcile your internal struggles.

And you can begin to enjoy this beautiful thing called life again.

If you've been asking yourself:

- Why the heck can't I feel pretty?
- How can I look good when I feel bad?

- What do I do with the clothing in my closet?
- How can I show off the things I love about myself?
- What am I going to wear today?

...You're here because you're ready to feel better than you have in a while.

You're here because you're ready to change something in your life. No, wait...you're not trying to change who you are. You are trying to bring a powerful and amazing person back to the world.

Stop hiding yourself behind clothing that doesn't make you feel amazing. Stop hiding yourself behind trends and ideas that aren't yours.

It's time to start unveiling the real you.

Even if you don't know who that is. Yet.

Remember, I am not going to dictate style advice to you through pictures in this book. I am not going to tell you that you have to dress like this or that in order to look great. What I am going to do is teach you how to style yourself. I will teach you how to find it in yourself to dress your best, whether you can afford to buy couture or you're on a Wal-Mart budget. Great style has absolutely nothing to do with how much money you spend on your wardrobe. Great style has much more to do with how much you **invest in yourself to be yourself**.

2

The Power of STYLE,
The Power of YOU

"The most courageous act
is to think for yourself. Aloud."

Coco Chanel

Right now, look at what you're wearing. Are you doing all you can to show off who you are? If you're honest with yourself, chances are good you're just wearing what you have around or you're wearing something because you think someone else wants to see you wear it.

It's sad, isn't it?

Style is supposed to be fun. When you put on an outfit, you're supposed to feel better, as though you're putting on something that accentuates who you are and what you have to share with the world.

But today, we're so inundated with what we're 'supposed' to look like that we forget to ask ourselves what we really want, and who we really are.

It's hard. I know it, and you know it.

Here's a secret: it doesn't have to be hard. You can be happy again when you walk into your closet and choose an outfit. What you need to do is rediscover who you are and what you want to express.

You need to find your power again...

Even if you didn't realize it was missing.

Where Did Your Power Go?

Once upon a time, you were happy with what you looked like. You put on a shirt and you smiled because it was your favorite. You didn't care if it went with your jeans or if it made your butt look smaller before you left the house.

Of course, that was way back when you were five years old and getting dressed for kindergarten.

But maybe you innately knew everything you needed to know about life before kindergarten. You were actually born knowing the basics of living a happy and self-confident life:

- Do what makes you happy.
- You are perfect no matter what.
- Boys are stupid.
- Smiling is more fun.

You didn't think about what others thought. If someone made fun of you, you hit them; they cried; adults made you apologize, and a few minutes later you were playing with them again.

Things were so much simpler when you were a kid.

You didn't think about your power because you always had it. You only said and did what made you happy. You did what you wanted because it was what you wanted.

No worries about anyone else.

No worries about how your decisions might affect someone else.

You just did what you did because you wanted to. When was the last time you felt this way about yourself?

Now, I'm certainly not suggesting you should just run around and do EVERYTHING you want.

What I want you to do is reclaim your power. I want you to rediscover the sixth sense you were born with that knows what it takes to make you happy.

Power is the sensation that rises up from your gut and fills your heart with the truth. Your truth.

Your powerful truth is the feeling that:

- You can do anything.
- You can succeed at anything.
- You were born with great instincts.
- You are perfect the way you are.
- You can use your powerful truth to style yourself.

Now, let's talk about power, what it is, and how it will help you discover the innate style that's buried inside you.

The kind of style I'm talking about is the style that makes you uniquely special. This is the style that will make YOU – not only your outfit - turn heads wherever you go.

A woman who is powerful is one who exudes strength and confidence, and her style is one of her best accessories.

What Does Your Power Look Like?

Power comes in a variety of sizes and shapes, depending on the person. While it could be easy to say that everyone has a certain je ne sais quoi, defining it is more of a challenge.

And that's really okay.

Instead of trying to box your power into something that looks fashionable, think about how your power would look if it were sitting beside you right now. Because it is.

Just as a fashion designer sits down and sketches the clothing they envision, so should you begin to sketch out the power that is inside you, waiting to be released. This power is beautiful, strong, and exciting. And you already have it.

Even if you think it's gone.

Designing Your Power

Your power is a sketch in your mind right now. You know what it looks like, you know what it feels like, and, most importantly, you sense what you will feel like once you try it on.

How long has it been since you tried on your power? How long has it been since you stopped thinking about 'someday' and started thinking about today?

Now is the time to bring your ideas into reality, invite them in, and allow them to take shape.

- **Find Inspirational Pictures**

  Whenever you are thinking about power and fashion, it's a good idea to look at pictures that inspire you. Find pictures that represent what power looks like in your life right now, or how you want it to look. This is a time to dream about the images you want to attract to your life, through what you wear and how you wear it. Look at magazines, the Internet, and any other sources of beautiful images. Do you have a friend or relative who exudes the type of style you love? Set aside photos of them, or ask them to pose for sentimental reasons. At this stage, it's up to you if you tell them why you want their photo. Keeping things private helps you remain your best confidante until you're ready to reveal your goals. Collect various images and place them in a file.

- **Find Pictures of Yourself**

  Another way to bring the image of power into your mind and life is to find pictures of yourself; but not just any pictures. Look around your computer and your photo albums for pictures of times when you were your most powerful. Maybe they were when you were younger, or at a formal event. Maybe you were posing for your Kindergarten class photo. Try to find at least one photo where you felt confident; no matter what you were doing at the time. Collect these pictures to add to the file.

- **Describe Your Feelings**

  Spread all of the images on a table or on the floor. When you look at them, you will begin to feel yourself shift and change from within. You will begin to see what power looks like. In this moment, take just a minute or two to write down and describe what this looks like, and more importantly, what it feels like. There are no right or wrong answers. Your honest feelings are the best answers.

- **List Words That Feel Powerful**

  Create a list of words that mean power to you, or make you feel powerful. Some ideas include: commitment, hard work, discipline, strength, balance, beauty, glamour, etc. Make it as long as you want, and only include the words that signify 'power' to you.

- **Think of Other Words You See As Powerful**

  Of course, it's not just images that make you feel powerful. There are different situations in your life that can also be powerful, *i.e.*, walking into a boardroom and making a presentation, making a bold move in a relationship, telling a waitress your order is wrong, calling a bill collector to tell them they made a mistake, returning a purchase that broke, quitting a job you hate, and admitting you made a mistake. Start thinking about times when you've felt powerful and add them to your list.

- **Design Your Power**

  With all of these powerful feelings and ideas in your mind, take out a piece of paper and sketch out what you think and feel. It's not supposed to be a work of art. You are not going to be graded. Take a few minutes to draw the powerful images that you feel and see when you look at the pictures and words you have collected. How is the person standing in the photo? What is his or her body language like, and what does it say to you? How is his or her head positioned? Where are his or her eyes looking? Is she or he smiling? How is she or he holding or gesturing his or her hands? To keep it simple, just draw a stick figure doing the same things that you observed. YOU are the stick figure. This is the beginning of the new you.

Finding Form For Your Power

If you're not interested in drawing anything out, there are other creative things you can do.

Far too often, we live in our heads and we over-analyze things. We believe that if we just think and analyze about things enough, we'll find the answers we've been looking for. And while this might work for logical problems, this isn't the right way to go about working on things that are less concrete.

Some may think the number of pounds you can lift measures power; but it's different when you're thinking about personal power.

Here are some other ideas to begin to find form for YOUR power:

- **Create A Vision Board**

  It's collage time! With the pictures you collected, make a collage of the images that make you feel powerful. This is a fun and easy project that will remind you how you want to feel and how you might want to change your style as a result. Feel free to post your vision board somewhere you will visit often. Keep it in a private place if you're not ready to invite others' opinions yet. This is about YOUR dreams, YOUR goals, and YOUR vision. It's not about getting approval from anyone else.

- **Get Some Clay**

  If you can't find or don't want to use clay, try to find good ole-fashioned Play-Doh. Make something that will help you feel powerful. There is a lot of power in making something out of a piece of nothing. Create a shape that makes you happy and reminds you of strength. A pyramid is a great one. Make it in your favorite color of

Play-Doh. Sit it on your desk, or on your bathroom sink, or mount it to the dashboard in your car.

- **Make Something – Anything!**

  You might want to make something you can wear right now as a reminder that you are committed to finding your power. Make a simple piece of jewelry, maybe a beaded necklace (or buy one), and wear it every day. Even a child's sillyband can be used as a daily reminder of your goal.

- **Do Something!**

  Doing something that makes you feel strong is what this is all about. Some people like to exercise because it makes them feel good. Doing something like yoga or running around the block might remind you what power feels like and how you might be able to create the sensation of power in your body more often.

These exercises don't have to be done all at once. You might not choose to do any of them at all. No pressure here.

But when you're struggling with finding your power, it never hurts to try different tactics to help rediscover it again.

And it's much easier than coloring your hair a wacky new color.

And far easier to maintain.

Visualizations For Power

The best tool you have for finding your power and strength again is your mind. In your mind right now, you're already cooking up the plans that will help you become the stylishly powerful person you already are.

In your mind right now is an image that you hold close to you--
an image that you may not have shared with anyone else.

This is the REAL you. The 'you' that you are deep inside.
We've covered how to reveal this image by using physical
methods, but now we need to shift your brain.

Did you realize that your brain is changing the way you feel?

Every time you think about anything, your brain takes a mental
record of it. And the more you think it, the more you believe
the record in your head.

It's sort of like your favorite little black dress, the one that you
turn to when you want to feel gorgeous. No matter what you
are doing, that dress makes you feel like a million dollars. Or
maybe it's a favorite pair of earrings or shoes that go with
everything. They always work no matter what.

The more you wear them, the more you've come to rely on
them. Actually, this is often the case with an entire wardrobe.
There are certain outfits that always make you feel good, even
powerful. So, you wear those outfits again and again.

To the exclusion of other amazing outfits in your closet.

This doesn't mean that you can't change things up, just as you
can change things up in your brain.

Your brain is just one of the parts of your body that doesn't
really enjoy change. It wants to stick with what it knows,
literally. Just as the more you walk on a path, the easier the
path is to find, that's how your thoughts work.

So, with this idea in mind, how you visualize yourself is the way
your brain pictures your power and your image in your mind.
Before you can be different, you have to reprogram yourself to
think differently.

If you've been thinking you're not powerful, or you're not worth the extra time this may take, or your self-esteem is so low there is no point in even trying, then you'll just continue to be that way unless you stand for change. I can't change you.

BUT...you can!

Changing Your Own Mind

You can change your mind. And you know this, but you might not have thought about what that actually means. You can CHANGE your mind.

To change your mind, all you need to do is:

- **Picture Yourself As Powerful**

  Close your eyes and try to see what you might look like when you're as powerful as you want to be. What are you wearing? What are you doing? Who are you with? How does it feel?

- **Imagine What You Look Like When You're Powerful**

  Stop and really think about what you're wearing – or would like to wear - when you're powerful. You might notice that you come back to the same image in your brain, again and again.

- **Imagine What Your Power Feels Like**

  When you have control over your own power, you are going to feel different. Close your eyes and think about what this feels like. Do you like it? Does it make you uneasy or nervous? Why?

OK, enough about thinking for the moment.

This is about practicing these powerful thoughts and re-programming your brain to focus *only on how you want to feel*, instead of how you don't want to feel.

Your brain is on your side.

It's time to take charge and tell your brain what you want it to do.

Choosing Your Power Again

You are powerful. Say it to out loud.

You are powerful. Say it again!

Power is a beautiful thing. When you make the CHOICE to have it on your side...you can do anything.

You may not fly from rooftop to rooftop, but you will choose to do big things. Things that you never told anyone else you wanted to do.

Simply because you've got the power to do them.

A New Playbook

Here we go! Now, it's time to rewrite your life and rewrite the rules you were going to follow for the rest of your life.

It's time to get rid of the old and welcome the new.

It's time to write your new plan.

You need to think fresh, think new. Don't think about the past. There is nothing you can do about that the past.

What can you do RIGHT NOW?

Because this moment is the only moment that matters.

Here's how you can write your own plan:

- **What you want:** You need to be brutally honest about what you want right this second. Whether it's just to look good or to feel better, you have to name it to claim it.

- **How to get it:** What should you do to get what you want? Chances are, you already know. You're just not doing it. Be brutally honest with yourself about what you need to do and how you need to do it.

- **What you will do:** Come up with a list of things that you will do starting right now. List things that will help you find your power. Promise yourself you'll do them from this point on. Write a contract to yourself, sign and date it.

- **What you won't do:** Some people think that power comes only from saying 'yes' to everything; that's not true. There's power in saying 'no.' When you say 'yes' too often, you give your power away. You give away the chance to show others who you are. When you're too busy being everything to everyone else, then you are powerless. It's time to say no.

Your plan can be fun! You could make an art project out of it, or a scrapbook of your before and after pictures.

You're beautiful today.

And when you own your power, you'll be even more beautiful...and stylish too!

Promise.

A New You

A new you is an exciting thing and it's coming right now. Actually, even if you do nothing at all, you will change.

How you change is up to you.

Every seven years, all of the cells in your body are replaced with new cells. Did you know that you are a completely NEW person every seven years?!

This is inspiring.

What's even more inspiring is that you don't have to do a thing to make it happen.

It just does.

You are renewed every seven years, even if you don't try or want to be.

Now that you're making the choice to change, you will see even better results.

The new you.

Introduce yourself when you look in the mirror.

- **Forget the past:** When you walk away from someone who mistreats, you don't look back. They don't deserve you. The old you who caused you to feel miserable doesn't deserve a second glance either.

- **Look ahead:** Keep looking forward. Notice the things that are coming up because now you're ready to give them attention. When you're driving, you control the direction where the car will go. Since you're the driver of your potential and your possibilities, you must look forward to direct your life in the right direction. You're in the driver's seat to steer your life to success!

- **Find possibilities:** Every day is filled with new possibilities. No matter how you may feel in this moment...every day could be an amazing day. If you get out of bed thinking this way, you will notice your entire attitude change. And you will watch doors open that were once closed. People will receive you differently because you are different. New opportunities will present themselves. All because you decided to look at your life as open to new possibilities, rather than closed.

- **Focus on the word CAN:** No matter what has happened to you, you CAN change. You CAN do more. You CAN be more. Use the word 'can' as much as possible in conversations, because you CAN do more than ever before.

The new you is exciting, bold, and waiting for more. I'm not talking about someone else. I'm talking about you.

The excited and bold person is YOU. And you've always been ready to take this step, to move in a new direction, and to be the powerful person you've caught glances of in the mirror.

Look directly into your eyes right now.

Admire the new you looking back.

When The Old You Speak Up

While I'm telling you to be bold and to be confident, I know better. I know that things aren't as simple as they seem.

I know there will be days you'll feel fat (even if you're thin) and days when everyone you meet is rude, or days when your spouse pisses you off, and especially days when your boss gets on your nerves.

And you'll wonder what's wrong with you.

There is NOTHING wrong with you. Even though you're reading a book about improving your style, it actually means you want to be better in some way. Even if you never changed a thing about yourself, you would still be amazing, stimulating, and gorgeous.

But the old you can be persistent.

You may start to feel like going back to the old you would be easier. Being bold takes energy. Being stylish takes time. Being gorgeous may not be what you already feel about yourself. You can't possibly see how you'll ever be powerful.

All that is NOISE in your head. It's noise because you're too comfortable where you are. That's how you got that way in the first place. STOP listening to the noise in your head! Create new noise.

In the first chapter, I told you this was not your average fluffy fashion book. I told you to get ready for a wild ride. Well, you're riding now! If you haven't gotten off yet, congratulate yourself for hanging in there. If you're still reading, then you're more than half way toward reaching your goals —for dressing your best — and BEING your best!

You need to take this next step. Because if you don't, you might find yourself powerless. You might find yourself waking up a year from now, wondering if life could be better.

> It can.
> It will.
> And you are in charge.

Style is about much more than how you're dressed, or how you look. Real style, effortless style is about who you are. It's the power that comes from knowing who you are, what you want, what you deserve.

But how can you stop the old you from taking over the new you?

- **Don't listen:** Although this may sound simple, it can be quite tricky. Stop listening to the doubts in your head. Stop paying attention to the negative noise. Just like you'd ignore a person you didn't like, stop listening to thoughts you don't like. Yes, they are your thoughts, but if they're not making you happy, what good are they?

- **Argue with yourself:** When you have persistent doubts, argue back. Stop letting your thoughts control how you feel. Argue with them. Break down the reasoning and point out to yourself why they are wrong. For example, if you keep telling yourself that others think you're unattractive, stop, and remind yourself of everyone who thinks you are attractive. More importantly, remind yourself of something you like about yourself. If the only thing you like about your body is your pinky toenail. Remind yourself that you have the cutest darn picky toenail in the world! If the only thing you like about your personality is the fact that you're a neat freak, then love how neat you are!

- **Get an outside opinion:** If you're feeling like you need help to stop listening to the old you, get another opinion. Get a second opinion from someone you love. They're going to tell you you're wonderful. They're going to tell you that you're amazing. Believe them. If you don't get a reaction that you like – YOU chose the wrong person. Go find someone else who says something you like! Surround yourself with ONLY positive people. Recycle your negative friends (and maybe even your negative family) with positive, supportive, loving, and happy people.

- **Break old habits:** Sometimes, changing to a new you means doing something the old you would have NEVER done. From changing to a new perfume to taking a new route to work, do something different. You are no longer the same person. So don't act like it! Clean out your closet, or start by cleaning out a junk drawer.

- **Get a theme song:** A fun way to remind yourself of your new you is to pick a song that makes you feel powerful. That's right. Stop and think of a song that makes you smile. Play it once. Then play it again, and again. Play it so many times until it's stuck in your head and you can't get it out. Whenever the old you tries to argue, sing the song or listen to it. Drown out the doubt. Let the music in your ears play louder than the negative noise in your head.

The old you will want to be friends again, but you MUST let it go.

You could always go back to the way things were. But the truth is, you'll be so happy that you changed your life and the way you feel, you will never want to go back.

Ever.

Fashion + Power = Strength

Now you know how to bring your power back. Or at least you have a better idea. The more you do right now to find your power, the more you will be successful.

So what does this have to do with fashion, or dressing your best?

A long time ago, gladiators wore armor to protect their bodies. It made sense at a time when fighters wanted to prevent injuries on the front lines of the battlefield.

Fashion is the same way.

When you put on a certain style or outfit, you feel different about how you look. Ancient warriors would intimidate their enemies by decorating their armour with different images.

As the enemy would approach, they would see the images and be scared off. Or that was the point anyway.

Your personal style can do the same thing.

You might not want to scare people away, but it doesn't hurt to scare your doubt away. In other words, arm yourself with your best self on the inside and outside of your body.

Bringing Power Back

Now that you've told the old you to get lost. You've decided to make changes. But nothing in your life has changed yet.

What gives?

While it might not seem like you're doing anything powerful yet, you are.

Just thinking about your life and what isn't working is helping.

The more that you begin to change your attitude, the faster you'll change your reality.

Want to know more ways to get powerful?

- **Smile:** It seems so simple, but a knowing smile is power. Just smiling at the world around you, no matter what, will make you feel better and it will make others want to know what you know.

- **Powerlessness:** A good practice is to think about times when life sucked. Think about times when you felt powerless. Think about what you were wearing in those times, what you were doing, etc. When you look back, can you see a pattern of actions you did, or people you associated with? You probably will if you look hard.

- **Avoid the power suckers:** Get away from those people who are energy vampires. People who just want to make you feel bad are not worth your time. They are simply trying to make themselves feel better about themselves by putting you down. As I said before, you need to be around healthier, more positive people.

Grabbing your power takes courage and it takes commitment.

This is a road that might not end in a day, a week, or even a year. But it will arrive at its destination.

And when you are there, you will be the one to enjoy the view.

And you will know that your own two feet got you there.

Cleaning Your Closet

You need to get rid of your past.

Literally.

While you might not think your past is something that can disappear, I want you to try. Sometimes, it's not about forgetting. It's about knowing what to avoid or eliminate from your life.

Take physical action that will let the past go.

The easiest way to do this is to get rid of excess stuff in your closet.

Not only is this a symbolic way to get rid of powerless style, but it's also going to make room for all of the good things you want to have in your life.

Don't believe it?

Think about a breakup you had. Yes, we've all been there. When you found something they left at your place, you got rid of it.

As soon as you did, it was like they were gone for good.

Removing objects with negative energy opens up your positive energy and wakes up your personal power.

Make time to go to your closet and to begin to think about ways that you can clean it out.

Set aside some time where you can turn up the music and have FUN with it. Crank up the volume, get a drink (unless you're letting go of that too), and start cleaning your closet.

Really cleaning out the cobwebs – emotional and physical.

You're not throwing out your clothes. You're making ROOM for your powerful style to come back home!

Here's how to make cleaning your closet something that revs up your personal engine and stokes the fire of your power. You have the spark, now it's time to get things heated up.

- **Lay it all out:** Get to your closet and start pulling things out. Lay them on your bed or on chairs to get everything out of there.

- **Clean the closet:** Just as you're getting rid of negative thoughts, cleaning your closet will help. Take a vacuum, a broom, and whatever else you need to use to clean out the closet. You don't want to put your clothes back in a dirty space.

- **Look at patterns:** As you look at your clothes, notice consistent patterns and colors. What kinds of clothes do you wear? What do you see in your work clothes vs.

your play clothes? You may notice that tend to choose clothing by your mood, or occasion.

- **Find your favorites:** Take a look at the things you wear again and again. Most people wear about 10% of what's in their closet. They don't really wear anything else. Why? We like what we like. But when you look at what you like, do you see stylish and powerful outfits? Or are your outfits hiding you from the world? Is everything black? Is it all basic? Has it gone out of style? Be 1000% honest with yourself here. If you haven't seen a style anywhere in the world except your closet in the past two-years (and it's not a basic layering item) it's time to bid it good-bye.

- **Remove what doesn't fit:** Yes, we all have skinny jeans in the back of the closet, but when you hang onto these, you're hanging onto disappointment. Really. When you look at those jeans, do you feel good? Probably not. Yes, it would be great if you could fit into them. But if you can't, they're useless. Get rid of things that don't fit. Give 'em to charity, or have a yard sale and make money off of them.

- **Remove unused clothing:** If you haven't seen a style in two years, or you haven't worn something in six months, chances are good you never will. It's just taking up space and it's not helping you. If you were going to wear it, you would have by now.

- **Get rid of 'someday' clothing:** Someday clothing is clothing that you thought you might need...someday. But if that day never comes, it's just taking up space that could be used for more important things. Like cool clothes that make you feel hot!

Your closet cleaning might take a day. A week. A month.

And you might have a lot of trouble getting rid of things. Some people have a lot of trouble getting rid of old clothes. Even I do!

Especially when they have sentimental value.

But you need to do this.

This is a process that's creating momentum for bigger changes. And while it might seem like a big change, it's only the beginning.

Clean out your closet. Make room for all that is to come.

Preparing for Battle

This is a fight in a certain sense. You are fighting to be the powerful person you know you can be.

The person you already are.

You need to prepare for battle and march into your life, confident that you can do anything.

Your closet should be filled with positive outfits and items. You should feel like anything you wear will help you feel amazing.

You should feel like you can do no wrong.

You are powerful, beautiful, and ready for the battlefield.

Let's watch what you can do now.

3

Seven Steps
To Dress Your Best

Reclaim Your Power Through Fashion

You can reclaim your power through fashion and personal style.

Instead of just looking for what's "in fashion," this is about wearing things well. You probably already know someone who does this.

No matter what they wear, they look fabulous.

You look at them and they amaze you. Even if they wear the same outfit or type of outfit every day, the fact that one outfit is worn proves how powerful and secure they are.

And you want to be like them.

However, you should only aspire to be yourself. Nothing is wrong with admiring others; in fact, we covered that earlier. Now that you've been there, done that, it's time to uncover the beautiful self within YOU. It's time to think about fashion, power, and how you fit in.

This is the day when you will finally transform every moment from this point forward. Let your transformation begin!

Step 1
Love Yourself No Matter What

Loving yourself sounds a lot easier than it is at times.

After all, it's easier to say you love a pair of shoes than it is to look yourself in the mirror and say I love you.

Until now.

The truth is, almost everyone is taught that it's selfish to admire, let alone love, oneself. We're taught that it's selfish to think about ourselves, about how great we are, especially for women.

So we keep quiet.

First, we stay quiet around others. We remain low key. It eventually becomes a habit. And before we know it, we're out of love with ourselves.

Sure, maybe you were once madly in love with your amazingness. Then someone said it was conceited to think that way, or they said you were full of yourself when you complimented yourself out loud.

So you stopped.

And when you listen to the world, you hear all of the reasons why you shouldn't love yourself. You hear the noise!

Too many things are wrong with you. After all, it's even more obvious if traditional media is to be believed.

And you do believe it. It's OK, most of us do.

Admit it.

But once in a while, when no one is around, you realize that love is a pretty cool thing. You're happy to love someone else.

You're happy when you're in love with someone else. You prance around singing songs with lyrics like "he completes me," and blah blah blah.

What about YOU? What about YOU?

Loving yourself is something that no one can take away. Ever. And you just need a push.

I feel so strongly about this that I have raised my 6-year old son to hopefully love himself so much that nothing will ever threaten it. After he says his prayers every night, he has learned to say "I'm great, I'm really great, and no one can take that away from me because I love myself and I choose to be happy, and I'm a leader."

As you sense yourself falling in love, and all of a sudden you see yourself with new eyes, it's at that moment when you can see yourself exactly as you should.

You can love yourself, whether you're in love with someone else or not.

You can love yourself, no matter what anyone says.

You can love yourself, no matter what anyone thinks.

You can love yourself, no matter what you think.

You might wonder if a pair of shoes could make you feel loved. If you finally had that gorgeous pair of $1500 Manolo Blahniks you would be complete. It's not that simple, honey.

You grow out of shoes, and out of the styles of the season.

You can't grow out of yourself. You and your body are here to stay.

You need to get to know the you that deserves love EVERY SINGLE SECOND of every day.

> No matter if it's a fat day.
> No matter if it's a zit day.
> No matter is it's a bad hair day.
> No matter what your friends ... mother... boyfriend ... boss ... celebrity ... or the media say.

Falling in love is easy. When you know how.

Can You Feel The Love?

Love is the eternal mystery. While it seems to happen overnight at times, it's actually a feeling that seeps into your soul when you least expect it.

Just believing in love allows you the chance to have it.

Lesson #1 – you can love yourself.

How can you feel something you can't see? You already know the answer don't you?

Love is:

- Those butterflies in your stomach.
- The feeling that all is right with the world.
- The notion that everything is perfect.
- The sensation that any choice is the right choice.
- The reflection in the mirror that smiles back.
- Not wanting to turn away from what might happen next.
- Feeling as if it will last forever.
- Wanting it to last forever.

You've been in love before. Whether it was with a person or an idea, you knew you were in love.

Even when you couldn't define it, you knew you were in love.

And you loved being in love.

You loved:

- Feeling lighter.
- Feeling calm.
- Feeling excited.
- Feeling energetic.
- Feeling beautiful.
- Feeling as if everything was going to be all right.
- Feeling understood.
- Feeling complete.
- Feeling loved.

When a lover looks into your eyes, you feel like someone is seeing straight into your heart. And while it might be scary, you enjoy it.

It's vulnerable to be in love.

There's a space between your blissful thoughts that reminds you – this could go away.

But you ignore it.

You avoid it.

Because the feeling you have when you're in love is so perfect that you only want to look at the feeling, and nothing else.

You want to wrap yourself up in the possibilities that come with being in love.

However, isn't loving yourself different?

No.

For one day, you need to look at yourself as being 100% perfect. No matter what you thought in the past, break up with that part of you that only has negative things to say.

Think of yourself as a lover who longs for another minute, another second to be with you. But that lover is you.

Close your eyes and think about how it would feel to ALWAYS be in love.

Enjoy this moment. Savor it. Believe in it.

Unlike the ones who love us, you can always — and only - count on yourself to love you. When someone else loves you, you're at the mercy of their feelings, their opinions, their judgments, their moods, and their approval.

Which can change. Quickly.

With yourself, you're never alone. You always have the choice to love.

You can fall in love again and again.

For one day, think only about all of the things that you love about yourself. We all have a list.

Your list might include:

- Your sense of humor.
- Your intelligence.
- The way you laugh.
- The way you look when you wake up.
- The way you look when your makeup is smudged.
- The things you've done.
- The risks you've taken.
- The boldness of your style.
- The way you love your children.
- The way you love your spouse.

Right now, figure out what makes you someone so loveable that no one could turn away.

And love yourself the way you deserve.

This feeling is intense, isn't it? When you begin to admit that there are pieces of yourself you really do LOVE, you'll begin to feel a warmth rise up from your toes and into your chest.

Your smile spills forth, uncontrolled.

How can you begin to love yourself?

- **Congratulate yourself:** Every day, you do things that others can't do. Congratulate yourself. If you say things that others wouldn't dare say. Congratulate yourself. All too often, we want to point out how great everyone else is, but why not point them out in yourself?

- **Sell yourself:** Tell others what makes you special, if they don't already know. Don't hold back from shining. You are beautiful with beauty others might not notice unless you point it out. What are you waiting for?

- **Share your goodness with others:** You do great things. Let others know. When you finish a great book, or finish a 5K, tell others. Those accomplishments fill you up, but they get even better when you share them. Stop hiding and start glowing.

- **Ignore everyone else:** If someone else says something negative, ignore them. From this moment on, you will love yourself as though you're the only one that matters. If it puts a smile on your face, do it. Forget that anyone else is around. Chances are good they're thinking more of themselves than they are of you anyway.

Loving yourself is a process that may start slowly, but once you realize just how great you are, it's addictive.

You will begin to see that you have been holding yourself back.

And that just isn't going to cut it anymore.

You deserve more, so give yourself MORE.

Why We Don't Love Ourselves

Oh, this is too simple to answer, isn't it?

If there was a chapter that you could have written without my help, it would be this one.

All of us have been writing and rewriting this chapter – again and again. Even when we don't have the best reasons for doing it, we still think that we're not lovable.

We don't love ourselves for a number of reasons. None of them matter. Really.

Think about a person who's recently died. Their obituary talks about how great they were, even if they weren't.

Why?

Because we look back only on the good things in the end.

As depressing as this might sound at first, it's really about perspective. When we stop thinking about the ways we shouldn't love ourselves, we can begin a new chapter.

Before you're dead.

The reasons we don't love ourselves are many.
- Someone else doesn't love us back.
- Our mother told us _____.
- Our father told us _____.
- Family and friends said we were _____.
- We think we're not _____ enough.

- We believe that love is something that is given to us.
- We think that love is only in the movies.
- We believe that love is something that is selfish.
- We believe that we shouldn't.
- We don't want to seem full of ourselves.
- We're supposed to stay modest.
- We're afraid that if we loved ourselves, we would lose friends.

It makes me mad just thinking about it.

Millions of amazing people are out there, just waiting to be loved by someone. In the meantime, they're (maybe you too) wasting their lives looking for love on the OUTSIDE.

They think that others don't love them because there's something wrong with the way they are.

THERE IS NOTHING WRONG WITH YOU.

Don't flinch when you read that. Say it out loud right now.

"THERE IS NOTHING WRONG WITH ME!!!"

No matter what anyone else says. No matter what anyone else thinks.

There is nothing, absolutely nothing that isn't loveable about you.

It's time to fight the idea that you're not absolutely amazing and wonderful and loveable.

- **Ignore the media:** While there are a lot of good intentions in the media, you do not have to listen to all of it. Waifish anorexic models? Don't feel the need to become that. Listen to someone who knows YOU better. Um, that someone is you!

- **Stop taking advice you don't agree with:** You're constantly being blasted with ideas about what you should and shouldn't do. If something doesn't make sense to you, don't listen. You don't have to. But if something makes sense, listen. Listen to what makes you happy and what makes you feel loved.

- **Wear things that make you feel good:** Styles change of course. What makes you feel good may not. When you are feeling less than loveable, it's time to not only change your attitude, but to also change your outfit. Wear what makes you feel lovely. Even if it's the same pair of jeans you've been wearing for a week.

- **Smile:** A smile is something that never goes out of style. When you smile, your brain automatically turns on the positivity. You will begin to feel your mood lighten, your complexion brighten, just from smiling. Try it.

- **Argue with yourself:** Whenever you start listening to the voices and noises that make you feel less than happy, argue back. Tell yourself that you are loveable. You ARE in love with everything you are. And you're in love with everything you're not. It's all good. It's all you.

- **Stop anyone who wants to bring you down:** If you've been hanging around people who are telling you that you're not good enough, get the heck away from them. They aren't worth your time. You wouldn't stay hang out with a friend who constantly told you that you're ugly, would you? Tell others to knock it off. Or get away. Or both. Delete them from your cell phone. Detox all negative friends and influences from your life!

This is the time to stop listening to everyone else. No matter how good their intentions.

Your mom might want to make sure that you know all of your flaws so you can fix them.

But it's not about her.

It's about you.

Loving yourself means forgetting all of the reasons why you shouldn't.

Just like being in a relationship, you ignore all of their flaws (at first, anyway) because you LOVE them.

You need to treat yourself the same way.

Sometimes people want to make themselves feel more loveable...by telling you that you aren't, like it's a contest or something.

It's not.

Well, there is a winner, and it could be you.

You just need to be the one to listen to yourself and ONLY yourself. Anything else is just background noise.

Anything else that makes you stop loving yourself is a pain in your behind and should be kicked to the curb with those 1980s acid-washed jeans.

Yes, there are many good reasons to be doubtful.

Well, not good reasons, but maybe logical reasons.

- No one is perfect. Neither are you.
- No one is going to look like Angelina Jolie. Except her.
- No one is going to look like Denzel Washington. Except him.
- Be YOU.
- You have things you regret.
- You are worried about the future.
- You've had love and lost it.

Maybe there are reasons you could doubt yourself. No one does everything right.

It's impossible to be everything we want to be all the time.

But that's not how love is measured.

Love isn't a measure of logic or the number of points you gain each day. It's the constant reminder that love is free. Love is something you can give yourself, even when things are horrible.

Even when you think life is impossible, there's always love.

You can love yourself.

Be the best friend for yourself that doesn't leave your side. No matter how bad it gets.

You do it for your friends and family.

Why not do it for yourself too?

Love From Others

Love. Most of the time, it's something we only experience or appreciate when someone else loves us.

We think that when someone else sees something great in us, then it must be there.

But what happens when you're not in love? What happens when someone else doesn't tell you that they love you?

Does that mean you aren't loveable?

Sounds like 'if a tree falls in the middle of a forest and no one hears it, does it make a sound?'

Who cares?

Really.

People who say they love you should love you for YOU, not for any other reason. But the truth is, some people fall in love because:

- They're in love with being in love.
- They feel like you complete them.
- They want something from you.
- They want to make themselves feel better.
- They want you to love them back.
- They think it's 'time' to love you.

These are all horrible reasons to love someone.

That's why it's so stinkin' important for you to love yourself for who you are, without relying on other's opinions of you.

Just because someone else says they love you doesn't mean that you owe them anything or that you must love *them.*

You will end up disappointed if they ever stop loving you – no matter what the reason. Instead, you need to be the light of your life.

Instead of focusing on those around you, look to yourself.

You aren't going anywhere.

You can look to yourself to guide yourself back to sanity and back to something that's real.

This isn't to say that you can't trust others.

Not at all. What you should do is be willing to trust and love yourself, even when others do not.

They're not trying to hurt you, but they might if you let them.

On the other hand, when a person truly does love you for who you are, that's no bad thing.

- They remind you of your good stuff: A person who loves you will love you and tell you why. They will remind you of the good things you do and the great person you are.

- They will keep you positive: The more positive and loving people you're around, the more positive you will be. We always want to fit in, and this is a great way to give in to peer pressure.

- They can encourage you to love others: when you're with someone who actually loves you, you will share the wealth.

This is a cycle of love that can help you be even nicer to yourself, even as others begin to fall away.

And they will.

Many people in your life will feel one way one day and they will turn around and feel another way on another day.

That's just life. We can't control it.

But when you stop focusing so much on what others think of you and whether others love you, you will begin to love yourself.

And what happens?

- People will see that you should be loved.
- People will begin to wonder what you have to offer.
- People will begin to think of their own good stuff.
- People will begin to be honest with you.

It's true – love turns into more love and more love and more love.

While you wouldn't say that love is a weed, it's certainly just as persistent. Think about it.

When you love yourself, you will begin to be even more attractive. That will bring loving people to you, which will amp up your ability to love yourself.

And when that happens...the cycle can continue.

Again and again and again.

You care about what others think of you because:

- You want them to like you.
- You want them to appreciate you.
- You want them to notice you.
- You want others to love you.

These are all good things.

But when you start sacrificing how much you love yourself because you are waiting for someone else to love you, the insanity has to stop.

You're the one that can love yourself RIGHT NOW.

No more questions.

No more doubts.

You know you can trust yourself. And you can love yourself no matter what happens next.

Loving Yourself

Yes, you know what love feels like.

You know what you love about yourself. But what's the next step?

Falling in love with someone happens like this:

- You meet.
- You find out everything you can about them.

- You celebrate what's great about them.
- You spend time together.
- You continue to appreciate them.
- They appreciate you back.

And ideally, this cycle continues.

So, let's look at loving yourself in the same sort of way. You need to meet yourself first.

- **Find out what you like:** If you're not sure what you like, stop and think about what you would do if you had 24 hours to yourself. Plan out the perfect day. Then live it.

- **Find out where you're from:** Sometimes you can love yourself all the more when you find out where you're from. A little research into your ancestry can show you how far your family has come and how much more you have to learn.

- **Find out what your story is:** Writing out your own story, or a fairy tale, helps you begin to understand how you see yourself. Don't worry about being an amazing writer. This story is only for you.

Find out everything you can about yourself. In the process, you will begin to uncover things you didn't know – and that's pretty exciting, isn't it?

Even though you've been in your own skin your entire life, you can always find out more.

And next, you celebrate yourself.

- **Do things you like to do:** This sounds so simple, but when you think about it, how often do you do things that you and only you like to do? Not very often, probably. Stop and do only things that you want to do for ONE WHOLE WEEK. If you're not in love with yourself by then...try it for another week.

- **Celebrate milestones:** When you have a birthday, you might count on others to celebrate, but what about you? Celebrate yourself. You're worth it.

- **Celebrate achievements:** Did you do something (else) amazing? Take yourself out to dinner. Bring friends if you like, but make sure you celebrate you. That way, your good deeds are never unnoticed.

This doesn't have to end here. You can appreciate yourself even more each day, allowing love to blossom.

- **Write yourself love notes:** Yes, writing a love note to yourself is a great way to remind yourself of your own love. Stop and think about what you love about yourself and address note to yourself. Place it somewhere you will find it later in the week. Repeat as often as you like.

- **Capture pictures of yourself:** You have pictures of lovers, but what about yourself? Take out your cell phone or camera and take pictures of yourself. Put them where you can see them. Smile big in the picture and show how happy you are with you.

- **Smile at yourself:** When you see yourself in the mirror, smile. You should be glad to see yourself when you notice your own face and body.

- **Tell yourself that you love you:** Tricky, but effective, each morning, look in the mirror and say that you love yourself. At first, you will be acting, but in time, you will believe it.

As you continue this process, you might find you're even buying yourself roses and chocolates.

Think of the beginning as dating yourself, but this is just the beginning of a lifelong friendship.

So to speak.

And you can date yourself forever. How great is that? No worrying about moving in with someone else.

You can be the perfect love for yourself.

Showing Love Through Fashion

But what does this have to do with fashion? Good question.

Here's the thing about style and your wardrobe, what you wear affects everything you do and everything you feel. While you might not realize it, when you dress well, you are showing yourself love.

It's like signing up for a massage.

When you do something special for yourself, you will feel better and you will begin to see that you are taking action to show that you love yourself.

Just as when a lover remembers your favorite song or gets you coffee when you want it, the more that you dress yourself well, the more you will feel and care for the love that is inside of you.

Remember when I mentioned the idea of dressing comfortably? There were no details there.

Why?

Because everyone is different.

What you need to remember right now about loving yourself through fashion is that what you choose to wear is unique. What someone else thinks is lovely to them...may not be lovely to you.

Jeans for you might be sloppy, but a little black dress might be just what you need to feel appreciated by yourself.

Here are some ideas to help you look like love (for yourself).

- **Wear a favorite outfit:** You know which one it is. It is the outfit that makes you feel HOT no matter what you're doing. And even if you just wear it to the grocery store, you should. Put on your favorite clothes and enjoy how you feel.

- **Know the colors you like:** If you're a person who likes black, wear it. If you like purple, wear it. Celebrate the colors that make you smile.

- **Accessories matter:** If you have a necklace that your grandmother gave you and it makes you feel loved, wear it.

- **Take a risk:** Sometimes, you just need to wear things that might not make fashion sense, but they make you happy. Forget about trends for now.

- **Wear clean stuff:** Loving yourself means respecting yourself too. Don't put on your dirty clothes. Wear something fresh that makes you feel amazing. Enhance it by spraying your favorite scent.

- **Press your clothes:** Wrinkles might not be a big deal, but if they make you feel frumpy, it's time to break out the iron. At least toss that outfit into the dryer to freshen it up. If you don't feel like ironing (which I never do), hang it in a hot shower and almost any wrinkle will disappear.

- **Try dry cleaning:** Think about treating your clothes with special care and you'll always feel pampered.

- **If something doesn't feel good, change:** If you look in the mirror and you don't feel the love, it's time to change your clothes.

You can love yourself, starting right now.

There's no better time to fall in love with yourself. Is there?

Step 2
Flatter Your Figure,
Forget Your Flaws

Your figure.

Admit it, you love it and you hate it. Some days, your body can do no wrong. You can look in the mirror, give your hip a shake and know that you're hot stuff.

But then there are those *other* days. The days when you wish your figure was anything but what it actually is.

You look in the mirror...quickly. Just enough to make sure your clothes match, but if you look any longer you see nothing but flaws.

Look, we all have flaws. Everyone. Yes, EVERYONE. While it might seem like some people are blessed with perfect bodies this is not the case.

Even Angelina Jolie and Denzel Washington have flaws.

What's the secret to looking like you don't have any flaws? Don't show them to anyone.

It's true. You can forget about your flaws, in the same ways that celebrities and their stylists do.

You can simply forget they exist – and no one you meet or see will be the wiser. Eventually, you'll feel flawless.

The Truth About Your Figure

Your figure isn't formed by anything more than the way that your bones are arranged.

Your figure is also the way that your genetics happened to blend when your parents got together.

If you can start looking at it like this, you might begin to be a little nicer to yourself. Most of the time, your genetic figure is something that's completely out of your control.

Well, mostly.

While you might want to get in better shape, this doesn't mean that your life should come to a standstill until you are 50 pounds lighter.

Heck no. Your life is still going on right now, whether there's a single or a double digit in your clothing.

(The last time you went out, did anyone actually check the size of your dress? Probably not.)

Your figure is going to have different features than others, and that's what makes you beautiful.

Imagine how boring the world would be if everyone was:

- Tall.
- Thin.
- Blonde.
- Blue-eyed.

This isn't to say that people who have these features are boring. However, if everyone was the SAME, this world would be dull.

You need to look at your figure as a part of the uniqueness that makes YOU special. And you are pretty darn terrific.

Your figure may have flaws in your eyes. But it's more important to spend on living in the present moment.

When you're focused on what you COULD be, you're focusing too much on tomorrow, on a someday that might never come. Focus on today.

What will happen if your body won't slim down as much as Gwyneth Paltrow's or Halle Barry's? Should that mean you shouldn't be happy in your life? Please say no.

You need to be happy no matter what you look like. And you can be. Even if you have to fake it until you make it, you'll start to enjoy and appreciate your body.

Your body automatically does amazing things all day:

- It breathes.
- It moves.
- It lifts things.
- It pumps blood.
- It can see the world.
- It eats.
- It drinks.
- It fights off disease.

And that's not all.

We take our bodies for granted most of the time. We think our bodies are something that should look great, and function a little – and nothing more.

It's sad, isn't it?

Our bodies are amazing – and not because we can squeeze into a 2.

Your body and your figure are just one part of who you are. And while you might not be completely happy with the way you look, that shouldn't stop you from being a style maven.

You can dress your figure to make sure that your body is as banging as possible — no matter what the scale tells you.

Toss that scale. It's the worst fashion accessory there is.

Different Shapes, Different Needs

When you're ready to forget your flaws, you still have to remember that your body is a particular shape and silhouette. Differences in shape mean that certain styles are accentuated more on some parts of your body than others.

So...

Every body shape should dress differently.

Women's body shapes include:

- Petite
- Curvy
- Curvy petite
- Large busted
- Small busted
- Short torso
- Long torso
- Straight waist
- Pear shape
- Apple shape
- Pencil shape

Now, before you start feeling bad about yourself, stop it. Every woman fits into one of these categories.

Every – single - one.

The way in which you dress your particular shape can make your figure appear more balanced than it really is.

Allow me to explain.

When you're apple shaped, for example, you shouldn't feel like you have to run out and work out until you pass out.

What you should do is look for techniques that make your silhouette appear to be curvier. It's all about proportions. And to be honest, fashion is all about smoke and mirrors anyway.

During the 1600s and during the Victorian era, an extremely narrow waist was considered to be the most fashionable and the most feminine. Corsets were designed that could reduce a woman's waist to less than 15 inches! Corsets didn't actually change the body; they simply forced the waist to look much slimmer than it was.

Appearances are deceiving aren't they?

No, you don't have to wear a corset, but you should know that many celebrities are wearing very tight girdles and supportive undergarments when they're out and about – even when they're just heading to the store.

Why? Because their appearance matters to the public.

Do you need to run out and get supportive pieces to make your behind or your stomach look flatter?

Well, you could.

But there are plenty of other ways you can make your body look better, without having a stomachache for the rest of the night.

There's nothing stylish about wearing some sort of girdle, not being comfortable, and then tugging at it for the rest of the night.

We're still keepin' it real here.

Here are some of my tried and true secrets for making one's body appear more attractive than it actually is. The more attractive you feel, the more comfortable you will be in your own skin...no matter what the magazines say.

- **Proportion:** When one part of your body seems to be bigger than another part or it doesn't seem to create a balanced shape, the sense of imbalance can tend to make you feel uncomfortable. Instead, balance your body by making different sections of your figure look as if they're about the same size.

- **Play up what you have:** If there is something about your figure that you LOVE, then why not make it more pronounced than anything else? There's a reason why Pamela Anderson wears low cut shirts ALL THE TIME. If you've got it, flaunt it. Confidence corrects figure flaws.

- **Play down what you don't like:** Yes, you might have a part of your body you're not in love with (yet). So, there are plenty of ways to play these bits down. You can make sure they're not the first parts people see when they look at you.

Your figure is going to have parts that you want to show off and those that you might want to keep neutral for a bit.

The good news is that no matter what your body looks like right now, you can adjust it. You can make your figure look all the more attractive – without having to exist on carrots.

Just keep your goals in mind by choosing from the following, or creating your own wish list:

- Longer legs
- Slimmer waist
- Slimmer hips and buttocks
- Longer torso
- Longer neck
- Shorter arms

- Shorter waist

Create a wish list of what you want to look like when you get dressed in the morning. This process will help you to envision what you want to change and how you might begin to alter, enhance and update your style.

Fashion is as an illusion as much as makeup is on your face.

Think about your face for a minute. What is one of the first things you do before you apply eye makeup, blush and lipstick?

You cover up your flaws.

You apply powder to camouflage uneven tones, or you apply concealer and dab it on all of the little imperfections that you want to cover up.

They're still there, but no one knows it.

After a time, even you forget that you have those small flaws in your skin. Why? Because you're drawing the attention away from them to other parts of your face.

You're putting on eyeliner and mascara or a bright lipstick. When you do this, you create the best possible version of who you are and what you have to offer. You're ignoring your flaws!

This is beauty.

This is style.

What you have may be what others want anyway. Check out the way your body curves. Women without curves surely want what you've got!

The way that your chest is flatter than you'd like? Some woman out there wants your chest because they think theirs is too big.

Do you have curly hair, but you wish it was straight? Have you noticed how often millions of women over process their hair to try to get it to be as curly as yours is naturally?

Do you hate your bone straight hair, and you really wish it was curly? Millions of women all over the world pay hundreds of dollars for relaxers to get make their hair look like yours.

Are your lips thicker than you'd like? What about the latest trends in lip injections and lip implants? People are willing to endure serious pain, and pay thousands of dollars for it – just to inflate their lips to look like yours.

It's sad, isn't it? We all want what we don't have.

Instead, I say we should begin to appreciate what we DO have. This section is meant to stop you from using the word "flaws" whenever you're talking about things you don't like about your body.

Because they're not flaws.

If there are things you want to change about your body, you probably want to feel more confident as well. And if that means you dress to make your waist look all the more slender, then I say go for it.

If you don't feel 100% confident in how you look right now because you're not 'perfect,' it's time to rethink the way you dress and the way that you present yourself to the world.

You are perfect just the way you are.

However, there's nothing wrong with enhancing your features to make them look even more perfect.

Here are some things you need to know about your figure:

- **It's unique:** Your body is your body is your body. And that's pretty amazing when you think about it. You might look like your family, but your body is still uniquely yours.

- **It will change:** Your body is going to change. Gravity happens and aging is something that starts no matter how well you eat. Your body is going to change. Let it.

- **You can make changes anytime you want:** If you want to lose weight, go for it. If you want to dress in loose clothing, do it. You are the one who's in control of the way your body looks to the rest of the world.

In the end, how you look IS under your control.

And if you're not feeling confident in what you're wearing, it's time to take control back.

Be the gorgeous woman you are.

Forgetting Your Flaws

Focus on what you have. Sounds simple, but it isn't.

We live in a world that wonders what ELSE you can have. We live in a world that's always thinking that the grass is greener on the other side.

Even when our grass is just fine, thank you very much.

Forgetting your flaws sounds like nonsense, like a silly New Age dream that is nice when you're in a seminar with someone with pink tights. And after you get home, you realize just how tricky it is.

Your flaws are there. Yeah, so what?

You can forget about them by focusing at what you already have.

Close your eyes right now and think about all of the things in the room around you that are red. Stop and really think about all of the things that are in the room around you and make a mental list of what's red.

Now, open your eyes and make a list on paper of all the things that are blue.

Harder to do, isn't it?

When you're looking for a certain color, you find it easy. But when you're told to look for something that you weren't focusing on, it became harder to do.

Your brain focuses on what YOU tell it to focus on. If you want to focus on something good, then you'll focus on the good. If you focus only on your flaws, then flaws are all you're going to see.

You've got to change your mind.

You can change your mind to focus on all the good things about your figure.

- **Change your attention when needed:** When you find yourself focusing on all of the things you want to change about your body, STOP. Think about your list, about what others have told you, and compliment yourself on what is truly hot about your body. The more you do this, this easier it becomes.

In time, your brain is going to focus only on the HOT spots that you have. When you look in the mirror, you're going to see someone who is absolutely gorgeous and amazing.

Because you are.

Because you ARE.

Stop thinking so much about what you need to change and what needs to go. You might lose weight someday...and you might not.

Why wait for your life to begin until things are perfect?

You have better things to do, don't you?

Techniques to Flatter Any Shape

Want to know how to make jaws drop when you enter a room? Yes, there are many ways that you can make people see the beauty that you know.

And you won't have to buy new clothing, if you don't want.

(But that never hurts)

Here are some tips for every body type. By following these tips, you can enhance what you have and forget your 'flaws.'

Petite

If you're shorter than other women, do you have any idea how often tall women wish they could be your height?

You are automatically more feminine looking, but you also know that you get 'cute' more often than you might want.

In either case, there are plenty of ways to play up and to play down your petite-ness, if you want to do so.

- **Go for one color:** When you wear only one color on your body, or similar shades of the same color, you create a longer look than you would if you break up colors. You will have just one line of color on your body. This is going to make you look taller and it will ensure that you don't 'break up' at certain points because of color blocking.

- **Wear clothing that fits well:** If there's a tip that women of all sizes should follow, it would be to wear clothing that fits. Try not to wear things that are baggy, hoping they will make you look different. Work WITH your size. Not against it.

- **Shop in the petite section:** Yes, if possible, it's better to shop in the section that has clothing for your shape. While it might be a pain to find these sections in the stores where you shop, there are many online shops too.

- **Get your clothing tailored:** If you already have clothing that's not 'petite,' then you might want to look into getting your clothing tailored. This will help you to create the sleeker look and smaller look that your body already has.

- **Look for shorter skirts:** When you add more 'leg' to your lower half, it will make you look taller. Try to allow more leg to show, where appropriate. And if this is uncomfortable for you, then stick with the same color of stockings as your skirt. When you do this, you will look longer.

- **Consider high heels:** Now, wearing high heels isn't comfortable for everyone, so if you don't want to wear them, don't force yourself. But when you want your legs to look a mile long, wearing higher heels (assuming you can walk in them) is going to help you look better than you might realize.

- **Think about turtlenecks:** For petite women, wearing turtlenecks creates a longer torso, especially when they match the color of a pant or skirt. These aren't for everyone, however. If you have a short neck, you should avoid them. But a classic black turtleneck sweater is going to look stylish, no matter where you are.

- **V-neck shirts and sweaters:** While this seems to be the opposite advice as a turtleneck sweater, some people find that the look of the v-neck makes them feel longer and taller. Try it. They're classic too and can work with dresses as well as t-shirts. They're great at elongating a short neck, or making a short figure appear longer by displaying more skin.

Petite women are faced with the problem of being too small, in comparison to 'normal' sizes.

Though this doesn't sound bad, it can make you stand out.

Instead of hiding your size, try to show it off.

Plus, you might want to remember that petite doesn't have to equal cute.

Sneak into the juniors department to find classic clothes that fit you well. Be careful. If you're not a teenager, don't buy clothing that reflect trends that juniors are wearing. Use this department to find a few classics instead.

While you might be able to find your size in the juniors section, do you really want everyone to think you're perpetually twelve years old?

Didn't think so.

Curvy

Too often, the idea of a curvy body is a double-edged sword.

Your curves are celebrated by men who love them and women who want them, but most designers don't carry silhouettes or sizes that fit your frame. I know this from personal experience. I'm 5 foot 3 inches, and I've had a J. Lo booty long before Jennifer Lopez was famous. I'm a fashion designer, and it's even hard for me to find clothes that fit my curves.

It's such a pain in my curvy ass!

Whether you're comfortable with your curves or you'd prefer to downplay them, here are some style tips you can use right now.

- **Try pinstripes and princess seams:** When you want to flatter or emphasize your curves, use lines and seaming. Coordinate them with solid pieces, and not patterns which will look too busy.

- **Vertical ruching is your friend:** If you have a smaller waist, look for tops and jackets with gathers that are directed pointing toward your waist. They help you to look smaller and curvier - in a good way.

- **Pointy shoes are a must:** Creating contrast with small pointy toes makes everything else seem smaller too. Ignore or discard ballet flats, and any shoe with a rounded toe. Sometimes trends that look good on someone else may not look their best on you. Know which trends to follow and which ones to ignore. This is one to ignore. I haven't worn a ballet flat since I was a ballet dancer in pointe shoes over 25 years ago. I only started wearing flats recently because my chiropractor made me. Too many years wearing too many high heels have finally taken their toll on my feet. My secret to healthy and stylish feet: I wear flats almost everywhere until I arrive at my destination. Then I quickly change into the high heels I've stored in my car or bag. I no longer care if I look "cool" on the subway or in a taxi, which actually makes me carry myself even more stylishly.

- **Straight lines:** Focus on wearing clothing that fall straight down your body. This will soften curves and help you look more clean cut. Of course, if you want to work the curves, GO FOR IT!

- **Trousers for everything:** Well fitting trousers, and jeans, etc. The fluid line of pants that fit well make your legs look long and lean. Pair them with high-heeled pointy shoes and your legs will rival a model's.

- **Halter top dresses:** If you're heading out for the night and you want to accentuate your girls, why not opt for a halter dress with some cleavage? It draws attention to your face and to your slim neck.

- **Don't go for super high heels:** Yes, high heels can cure many style woes, but when you're not comfortable walking in them, this is going to cause you to look un-chic. Only wear them if you can walk in them with ease. Nothing looks worse than a woman who's wobbling to the car in platform heels. Oh yea, what's worse is women who take their shoes off to walk barefoot at the end of the night. THAT will never be in style!

- **Black slims:** No matter what others have said, black DEFINITELY slims. If there's a part of your figure that you want to camouflage or downplay, wear black in that area, or in the whole outfit. Black always works and it always looks good, no matter the season.

- **Three quarter length coats for work and play:** Again, you want to create structure around your body in order to forget any flaws. When you wear a long coat that's about ¾ the length of your body, you won't overwhelm your figure, and you will create a sleek line. Look for thicker, dense or sleek fabrics to enhance the coat.

- **Short box cut jackets:** This cut helps keep your upper body tucked in, so to speak. They also make curvy bodies look longer.

- **Try a skinny belt:** If you have a smaller waist, try adding a slim belt to your outfit, when possible. This will draw attention to your small waist and help your curves work for you.

- **Knee high boots work well:** When you're taller with curves, wearing knee high boots over skinny jeans or leggings can style things up without making you look bulky.

- **Follow your natural shape:** In the end, always follow your natural shape. Things can get out of hand whenever you try to fight your shape.

With these tips, you can shop anywhere.

And look good doing it.

Curvy doesn't necessarily mean that you're plus size. You might simply have the kind of bone structure that blessed you with a super slim waist wide shoulders and well rounded hips.

The classic hourglass figure Marilyn Monroe was known for.

Most women would kill for this figure, and you were born with it.

Watch how great you'll look with these tips.

Full Busted

When you were a teenager, you probably prayed for larger breasts. Heck, we all did.

But no matter what you did, no matter what you promised in your prayers, you didn't always get what you wanted.

Ladies like you were lucky enough to have your prayers answered.

A bigger bust can be a challenge to dress. Medium shirts are too small, but you might swim in anything that's too big.

What to do, what to do...

- **Don't wear tight bottoms:** While you might want to play up your slim legs, this actually makes legs look too skinny and the bust look too look too big. Remember, you're going for proportion here. Wear bottoms that fit well but not tight, and even add a little volume to your body to balance things out.

- **Wear a-line skirts:** An a-line skirt will flounce out a bit, giving your lower half some bulk, which downplays the size a larger bust.

- **Jackets rest on the hips:** When you choose a jacket, make sure it rests on the hips, not below the hips. This will help to ensure you look balanced in the torso area.

- **Jackets are your friend:** Yes, jackets work well to help pull in your chest, but also to help you look streamlined and professional.

- **Wide legged pants:** To create more volume (not bulk) in your bottom half, choose wide leg pants, worn with a bust-skimming top. They will help to prevent you from looking too large on top.

- **Support is essential:** If you have larger breasts, you need to invest in good supportive bras and other undergarments. There's nothing less stylish than a woman without the right undies. Your breasts deserve the best. Get fitted for a great bra at your closest department store or lingerie boutique. Support your Girls!

- **Layers:** It's not a good idea to layer your body on the top to add more bulk to that part of your body. If you're intent on layering, always choose thin layers to avoid adding unnecessary bulk.

- **Add interest to your bottom half:** A flowered skirt or patterned pant draw attention away from your chest and focus it the patterned part of your body.

- **Go dark on top:** Wear dark on top and brights on the bottom. This will help to make sure your body looks balanced. Of course, if your bottom half is larger, this technique may draw attention to it. Keep that in mind.

- **Try a scarf:** To draw the eye away from the upper half, enhance your ensemble with a bright scarf around your neck. It will pull the eye up to your face.

- **Simple jewelry:** Wear larger, simple jewelry on top. This way, the eye will focus on your jewelry instead of your bust.

- **Scoop necks:** The gentle scoop neck is the best way to dress a larger bust area.

No matter what you might think of your chest, wear it with pride!

Especially at work.

Some women like to play up the larger assets when they're out and about, but there are times when this can look sloppy.

Look in the mirror before you leave the house.

Your ample bosom is something to celebrate since it turns heads when you walk in a room.

However, when you're in a professional setting, put the Girls away for a bit with these tips.

Small Busted

On the other end of the spectrum are those women who tend to wish they had more on top.

It's a common concern, and nothing to be worried about. Flat-chested models are booked the most for the runway.

Not that you look like that. Of course.

While your first response might be to go out and buy an expensive pushup bra, you may want to try some of these tips.

These tips will make the most of the shape you have, and to make your body appear more in proportion.

Looks can be deceiving – and that's half the fun of fashion, isn't it?

- **Small shoulder pads:** When you want to create more balance in your body, you need to make sure that your upper body looks as large as your lower body. If you have a smaller bust, this isn't always the case. Try small shoulder pads in your suits to see how this makes your body more even.

- **Stripes:** If you wear patterns on your shirts, they will add depth and dimension to your bust by making your breasts appear to be larger than they are.

- **Fitted is your friend:** Though you might want to add a lot of layers to your upper body or flowy bits to your lower body, it's better to stick with well-fitted clothes. Anything that's too loose can look sloppy and it can make your body look out of proportion.

- **Straight jeans:** Wearing straight jeans will emphasize your natural smallness, which is in proportion to your upper body. If you have a smaller upper body and larger lower body, look for jeans that are fitted at the waist and hip.

- **Layers on top:** To add volume, you can do this literally by adding more layers to your upper body. However, you will want to use thinner layers since too many layers can make your middle look thicker than you may want.

- **Change up your neckline:** You can choose different necklines to help bring more interest to the bust line.

You might want to choose higher necklines as this will help to create a larger area for the eye to follow, or ruffles at the neck which frame your face instead of emphasizing your bust.

- **Strapless dresses:** Since you can get away without a bra or other undergarments when wearing dresses, why not wear something strapless? This will bring the attention to your face.

- **A-line skirts:** It seems that the a-line skirt can do no wrong, can it? They add more volume to your body in general. You will simply look like you are smaller on top and you are wearing a great skirt.

- **Color where you want it:** If you're ready to showcase your lower half, why not add some color? At the same time, if you have a larger lower half, neutral colors on the bottom and colors on top can be a good combination for you too.

- **Collars help:** When you want to create more bulk for your breasts, try adding collars to your shirts. They allow you to appear as if you have more weight up top, even when you don't.

- **Bright colors:** Yes, bright colors can be a great way to draw attention to your bust and to your upper body, which can create the illusion that you have a larger cup than you really do.

- **Turtleneck tops:** Turtlenecks create a clean look on top and they prevent the top part of your body from being cut off from the rest of it. You will be able to look as though your breasts are bigger and in proportion to the rest of your body.

- **Fun details around the neck:** Why not add fun details to the area above your bust line, to accentuate the area and to draw attention to your face? This creates more visual interest at the bust line, which makes it seem larger.

Yes, you might want to use a pushup bra from time to time, but it's always more comfortable to use what you already have.

That way, you are being yourself.

Just a slightly more impressive version of yourself.

Short Legs

Some women crave the long, lean legs that models seem to have.

But all of us aren't built that way.

Some women have a long torso and shorter legs, which can make them feel out of balance with the styles of the day.

You don't have to feel that way anymore.

- **Wear shorter tops:** Since you want to make your upper body look more in balance, you should wear shorter tops like waist length jackets (like bolero styles), and blouses, etc. Longer tops will draw attention to the length of your torso.

- **Layer your tops:** To make your upper body look more balanced, layer the tops you wear to bring more attention to your face.

- **Straight pants and skirts work best:** Since you want to make your lower body look longer, stick with straight lines that will bring the eye up and down the legs.

- **Boot leg pants and jeans for flair:** A straight pant is best, but if you want a little more style, add boot leg cuts to your wardrobe. When these pants go all the way to the ground, your legs will look a mile long.

- **Solid colors on the bottom:** Wearing the same color pants, skirt, shoes, and stockings or socks will help to extend your lower half even more. When you wear a brighter top, this creates a look of height too.

- **Medium to high heels extend your legs:** If you want to make your legs seem longer, wear higher heels. They create a longer leg and help to bring your upper body into balance.

- **Get things hemmed to the ground:** Whenever you can, make sure that your pants go all the way to the ground. This doesn't mean they should drag behind you, but you should go to a tailor to have your pants come as close to the ground as possible, while wearing platform or high heel shoes. This makes your leg seem longer.

Short legs might seem to be a fashion no-no, but they're very common.

There's always something that doesn't seem balanced.

Instead, look to create balance in your body – balance equals style and style equals power.

Wide Waist

With all of the stress of the world, it's really no wonder that many women are carrying a little extra weight around the middle.

Whether you've had children, gained a few, or you just haven't been blessed with an hourglass figure, there are a number of ways to draw attention away from this part of your body.

Do you want to look sleek? Make your waist look thinner.

And it won't require plastic surgery or a diet.

- **Wear what fits:** You don't want to look like a tent, so don't wear one. When you wear things that are too flowy, it can look like a mess. Focus on fitting your body.

- **Try a belt:** You can use a belt to create a waistline, even where there isn't one. Choose a smaller belt that wraps around your torso above your natural waist. This is a small part of your body that will make you look sleek. But don't wear wide belts. Those are a No No.

- **Jackets help, if they fit:** A single breasted jacket should hit above your hip and it should have no more than a two to three buttons to make your tummy look flatter than it actually is.

- **Skinny jeans are a No No:** While you might have slender legs, skinny jeans can make your middle look bigger and that's not what you want. At all.

- **Pants on the hips:** Sometimes, wearing pants that are slightly lower than your natural waistline will help. However, if you have an extreme muffin top (hey, it happens), you might want to...

- **Choose pants with a higher and wider waist:** You might want to choose a pair of pants that has a high or wider waist to pull in your stomach and make you look tragically thin.

- **The longer, the better:** When you wear longer pants, you will extend the look of your leg, which can make you appear to be even leaner than you might realize. You can wear high heeled shoes as well to help make this part of your body the sleekest part of your body.

- **Brighter tops:** Sometimes, wearing something that is brighter on top will bring more attention to your face. And that will take attention away from your waist.

- **Dresses work your waist:** Empire dresses and those with pieces that are slimmer around the area below your breasts are going to help you look thinner and thinner. This is the part of the body that is the thinnest, so if the dress falls from this area, you will trim yourself up, without having to starve.

- **A-line dresses are the best:** Yes, a-line dresses are the best. You can't go wrong with them.

- **Darker bottoms:** If you want to attract more attention to the upper part of your body, you will want to invest in darker bottoms, including skirts and stockings.

- **Slightly wider bottoms:** While really large pants, jeans, and trousers will make you look larger, you will want to opt for slightly larger bottom hems to create proportion in your body.

- **Don't go past your hip:** You want your shirts and your jackets to stay at or above your hip.

- **EXCEPTION:** Wearing a long and colorful coat over a darker dress will make you look thin and stunning. These coats should be in proportion to your body. Longer coats for taller women, shorter coats for more petite women.

- **Find a spot to emphasize:** If there's a part of your body that you like, make sure that's where you're attracting attention. This is going to help you feel more comfortable about any of your 'problem' areas.

- **Dark colors:** When you're just ready to make your tummy disappear, look to wear dark colors throughout your outfit. This will make you look thinner without making you look like you're trying to hide too much.

A supportive undergarment can also pull in your tummy, though they should be used rarely.

They hurt.

Really, they tend to be uncomfortable. And while you might want to look good, you don't want to end up hunched over with a stomachache at your next party.

Flaunting 'Flaws'

This is the place to finally flaunt your flaws.

Let's talk about it.

Why not flaunt what you have and say *&^% it to everyone else? After all, if you're confident in what you're wearing, others will want to know the secret behind your confidence.

And confidence looks great on every body.

Every day. Every season.

There are a lot of ways you can flaunt the flaws that you have and make yourself feel even better about your body.

So, if you're the gutsy type of gal who's willing to try something a little more daring in order to get past any body issues or concerns, here's what you can do:

- **Find one 'flaw':** Choose one thing that you want to stop obsessing about. Find the one thing that you've been trying to hide for years and start thinking about it again.

- **Dress it up:** Whether you think you have large hips or your stomach is a little less than flat, think about ways to draw attention to it. Even if this means wearing something a little tighter than you normally would, try to find a way to make yourself aware of your 'trouble' spot.

- **Look at the reactions:** While your mind might have created a really bad dream in which everyone points at you and laughs, this is far from reality. In fact, now you'll probably notice you get more attention and more compliments for the outfits you're wearing. And it's just going to make you feel even better about yourself and about your body.

It's true. Try flaunting your whole body.

In reality, you're probably the only one worried about what you look like. Everyone else is worried about what they look like.

They don't even give you a second look.

Oh, they might think about you briefly, but they probably don't care that much about what you're wearing or about what your waist measurement is.

So, why not take this one life you have and really enjoy what you're wearing and what you look like?

Think of new ways you can simply make yourself FEEL beautiful. There's nothing like a bright and genuine smile on your face to make you feel powerful.

> And pretty.
> And gorgeous.
> And courageous.

The time for you to take control of your style is now. I want you to CHOOSE to forget all of your "flaws" as quickly as possible.

They're actually what make you uniquely you. And while you may still try to trim down, you will continue to celebrate your body and all that it can be.

Reclaim your body's power by reclaiming what you look like!

Step 3

Dress for Yourself, Not Anyone Else

With all of these style tips — and all the ones you see in magazines — it's confusing to know the 'right' thing to wear, and what you shouldn't wear.

Wait...does it really matter?

The more that you look at the way that you've been thinking about your fashion and about your life, you might begin to see that power isn't about a certain designer label.

It's not about a size.
It's not about a color.

Your power and your style are all about making you feel INVINCIBLE. When you walk into a room, the way you dress matters, not because you're trying to meet some set of rules.

You're trying to make yourself remember and openly represent just how amazing you really are.

It can be challenging at times to dress for who you are, and how you want to feel.

With so many new situations and people, you might be concerned about who you are, what you are presenting to the world and whether you are impressing them.

It's natural to want to fit in.

But what would your world be like if you STOPPED thinking about what others thought of you?

What would your life be like if you simply lived your life as though nothing and no one else mattered? Would your closet change? Would your shopping habits change?

If they wouldn't, then you're already on the right track to your personal style and power. You already know what you like and, darn it, you're sticking to it.

But if you feel a little lost when it comes to how you dress and what you should wear when you're out and about, it's time to think about what makes you happy and comfortable.

Maybe wearing certain designers makes you happy.

> Great.

But you might also feel that certain styles or certain fabrics make you happy. And that's great too.

This style tip is designed to help you sort out what's you and what's not you. Somewhere in the middle, you will find the style that is uniquely you. This is the style that makes you feel the most powerful.

This is your style of living, which is the way you need to be...

> Happy.
> Content.
> Ready to take on the world.

Why Others Still Matter

It would be naïve to say that others don't matter when it comes to your style.

After all, when you buy clothes, you buy them because someone thought they were a good idea to make. You bought them because someone thought they were stylish enough to sell.

And you probably bought them (at least partly) to make someone else — in addition to yourself - think you look good.

We all do it.

It's okay.

What you need to keep in mind is that when you're looking at your style and reclaiming power, it's not ONLY about what others think.

However, sometimes it is.

There are certain situations where you normally wear certain kinds of clothing almost as if it's a social uniform:

- Work
- Family occasions
- Church
- The Synagogue and other places of worship
- Funerals
- Weddings

Most people wear certain things at certain places.

Does this mean you give up your right to look good? Well, no. Wearing a social uniform is just adhering to an image out of traditional respect for the purpose of the event.

You wouldn't wear a workout outfit to work.

Unless you work at a fitness center.

When you wear clothes that are in line with the purpose of your day, you are claiming your power no matter what you wear.

You are making the decision to follow the rules of the day and thus you are claiming the power that comes along with those rules.

- People will appreciate your choices.
- People will feel comfortable.
- People around you will feel respected.
- People around you will notice your courtesy.

You get the idea.

It's a good idea to "fit in" once in a while. And though you might change right into your own stylish (or comfortable) clothing as soon as you leave these occasions doesn't mean you are giving anything up.

Just in case you were wondering.

If you choose not to follow the pack, so to speak, realize it can be a good thing or a bad thing.

A good thing:

- **You will seem to be a trendsetter:** If you're in a group of creative professionals, for example, you will be the one who knows the trends of the day.

- **You will always be noticed:** When you don't look like everyone else, you will certainly be noticed, even if you don't mean to be. You will stand out in the crowd.

- **You will be the one who gets heard:** If you are a person who gets noticed, the chance that you will be heard when you are speaking is much greater. You will be the one with the great idea that gets implemented.

- **You will be someone who is exciting:** when a person stands out, they tend to seem more exciting than anyone else.

- **Yes, being different is a good thing.** And yet, there are times when it's more powerful to stick with what's expected.

A not-so-good thing:

- **You look out of place:** In a very physical sense, a person who doesn't dress like everyone else will seem as though he or she does not fit in. If you don't dress the part, you won't look the part.

- **You look like you can't follow directions:** If you're heading to a black tie event and show up in jeans, people are going to wonder if you looked at the invite.

- **You look out of touch:** When you're with a group of people who have always done things a certain way, any deviance will look like you're out of touch. Even though being unique can seem like you're 'in the know,' it can also be a double-edged sword.

- **You will seem like you don't belong:** You won't look like you're a part of the group or event if you don't follow "the rules."

- While rules are certainly made to be broken, it's often better to bend them than to completely break the ones that have been in place for a while.

  Rules, rules, rules.
  No one likes them.

And yet, they're still around for some reason. The times when you need to follow the fashion rules will be minimal.

You can return to your regularly scheduled style afterward.

How To Make Your Own Decisions

When you're new to style, or you're just ready to look at style in a new way, it may be hard to figure out what your style is.

After all, if you've never had your own STYLE, then how can you figure out what "your" style is in the first place?

This is the fun part!

This step is the tip that will help you not only uncover your stylishness, but you will also begin to find out what makes you feel the most powerful, the most alluring, and the most attractive.

Yes, it's time to release your secret diva!

Diva time should include a celebration of how beautiful you are inside and out.

Now that you know how to play up or play down your 'flaws,' you should start shopping for your style.

Either take a day for yourself at your favorite mall, or get situated in front of your computer for a few hours to shop online.

Whatever you do, and how ever you decide to do it, make sure it's FUN.

Here's what you're going to do:

- **Find websites that sell your favorite clothing lines:** Go online and search for the websites that have clothing you like. Or you can just browse every fashion website that you like in order to see what's available. Don't rest until you find at least two websites or stores that have a lot of clothing that you like. This doesn't mean you should go on a shopping binge (yet). You are simply looking to see what kinds of clothes appeal to you.

- **Seek out clothing you like:** You need to make it your mission to look for clothing that's best for you and your body. If you find that the traditional stores aren't doing it for you, go to some local boutiques or thrift stores to see what's available. You want to look and look until you find something that you HAVE to have. That's when you know you've struck fashion gold. If you can't afford it, keep searching for look a likes, which are called "knock offs" in the fashion industry. ABS and Zara International are knock off masters. Check them out for affordable alternative options to expensive high-end designers.

- **Print out pictures:** If you can, take pictures or print out color pictures from the Internet of what you've found. Focus only on styles and cuts that flatter your figure. Place them side-by-side and organize them according to style and category. This will allow you to build a "look book" of the things that will create your style and begin to make you feel more powerful in your life. Viewing your favorites together at once will allow your vision, your style to reveal itself to you. Notice any constant themes or trends. Do a lot of the images lean toward one color range or another? Are a lot of them similar styles like long skirts, or narrow pants, patterns, plaids, florals? Your style is now telling you what it wants to be!

- **Find a virtual model to try on your outfits:** There are now a number of online programs and phone apps that will help you 'try on' outfits at certain fashion stores. You will want to use these virtual models (using your exact measurements) to see if things will fit, how they will look, and whether a certain style works for your body.

- **Go try things on:** It never hurts to just get out there and try on as many outfits as you can. This will allow you to see your fashion develop right before your eyes. Find a favorite sales person who really knows the store, get their business card, and use them often. They'll love you even more! Call them ahead if you're in a rush, and they will help you then too! Which brings me to another secret...

- **Use the personal shopping department:** This is one of the best kept secrets in retail clothing stores. A personal shopper's job is to shop all over the store – just for you. They put you in a private lounge style fitting room that is normally completely cut off from the public, and it's often in a very luxurious setting. They give you VIP special treatment, often bringing you coffee and snacks. They bring you everything from clothing tailored to your body, shoes, handbags, and even accessories. And...it's ALL FREE! They get a commission from your sales, but YOU never pay them for all of their special VIP treatment. Almost all major department stores have a personal shopping department. Call up, make an appointment, tell them what you're going to be looking for. Show up, relax and have fun!

- **Look at fashion magazines:** There are plenty of fashion magazines at your local bookstore or grocery store, so take advantage of them. While you might not like everything you see in them, you will begin to see what stylists are putting together this season.

- **Look at fashion magazine websites:** Most major fashion magazines have an elaborate presence online, so take some time to review these sites as well. The more that you look, the more you will find that will appeal to you.

- **Start watching fashion shows:** If you have access to television online or via a cable subscription, it's a good idea to look at the shows that promote fashion. When you do this, you can begin to see what styles are available and then you can head to the show's website to see where their collections are being sold.

The more you can fill your brain with fashion, the more comfortable you will be with it.

Just like anything new, you need to learn before you can apply what you have learned.

Some people might be able to just throw an outfit together.

But if you're new to this, take some time to dive into the fashion world. Don't worry about sinking. The 7 Steps to Dress Your Best will always help you swim in this world!

You will have fun doing it and you might just learn something new about yourself in the process.

However, this process can be less than fun if you do a few things that you may have already done in the past.

We're breaking bad habits with this book, okay?

This is what you're NOT going to do. Repeat out loud, "I promised Stephany that I will NOT..."

- **Follow all the trends:** While you might think that fashion magazines are books to be treated with reverence, they're not Bibles. You shouldn't feel like you need to follow trends that don't look good on your body or that you think are plain ugly (jeggings, anyone?).

- **Believe everything you see:** Yes, you might think that everything you see in the magazines means that those pieces of clothing will look good on you too. They might, but you also need to remember that most pictures in magazines are airbrushed, digitally manipulated, and just plain lies. You can't Photoshop yourself in real life, so don't believe everything that pictures tell you. I was Photo-shopped by an expert for the cover of this book. Do you really think I wake up looking like that? Hell NAW!

- **Dress your body differently than it's shaped:** You might be tempted to just squeeze into the latest style because it's in style. There's nothing wrong with going to a store, trying something on, and then seeing what it looks like on you. However, buying something that just doesn't work for your body is not an act of power.

- **Believe there is a 'right' way to dress:** There is NO right way to dress. None. No matter what anyone says (even me), there is no one answer to the question of what you should wear. Don't fall for the okey doke!

- **Buy everything you see:** This is the one that trips most people up when they're trying to rediscover their style or create one. You might be tempted to buy everything you see in order to find something that works for you. Yes, you might find something that works for you, but you might also end up with a closet full of things that don't work at all. Be discriminating. Please use your new found power NOT to become a shopaholic. Remember, materialistic things like clothes will never make you happy, only YOU will.

When you're first attempting to discover your style, you should focus less on what you should wear and more on what will work for you.

Start creating your style by finding what you like and then seeing if it likes your body.

If it doesn't, move on.

There are plenty of other outfits in the sea!

Shopping Alone

A tricky part of discovering your own style is shopping alone.

Shopping is such a social event when you are younger and even more so as you grow up and start spending money.

> You want to be with others because it's fun.
> But it's not helping you find power through style.

When you shop with others, most likely...

- **You buy what they buy:** It's just human nature to do things that others around us are doing. While it might not even be conscious, you will simply buy what your friend is buying. After all, if you don't buy it, you might feel that you are saying their choices aren't any good — and vice versa.

- **You shop where they shop:** If you're shopping with someone else, you both need to agree on where to go. If you're not in the same sort of "style" frame of mind, this means that you will go places they don't want to go and they will go places you don't want to go. This might end with you buying things you don't like, based on their taste.

- **You listen to other's opinions too often:** Even if you think you can block out the opinions of someone else, you're still listening. Since they're right there with you, you need to listen or else you'll seem rude. Not an easy place to be. Now that YOU know what's best for you, unless your friend is a style setter, or you really trust the sales person, you should listen to and focus on your own instincts.

- **You believe they're telling you the truth:** No matter what the other person says, when you're out in public, you're going to believe what they tell you, or you're going to pretend to believe it. So you might put a hot skirt back on the rack that you actually LOVE, all because your shopping partner doesn't like it. Be careful. Friends don't want to hurt your feelings, so many of them will tell you something looks great on you, when it doesn't. Tell them your newly thick skinned can handle the truth. But, don't shop with anyone who is not positive and supportive. Remember what you learned earlier about deleting negativity from every part of your life?

- **You forget about what you want:** It's different when you're shopping with someone else. You think more about what they like than about what you like. You might even begin to forget and shop based on what they are buying and why they are buying things.

- **You dress for the other person's reactions:** It's true. While you might not admit it at first, you are shopping to see what the reaction of the other person is. No one wants to walk out of a dressing room and have their friend tell them they look hideous. So, you probably pick out things that you know the other person will like. Even if you don't.

But when you shop alone, you will begin to do something different:

- **You'll go only where you want to go:** When you have your own agenda, you don't have to think about where someone else wants to go. You will go only where you want to go. This is going to help you begin to create a unique shopping experience. And it's just more fun to go to stores you WANT to visit. It's empowering!

- **You'll buy only what you want to buy:** Instead of being influenced by someone else's shopping and spending habits, you'll buy only what you want – nothing more. Have you ever been to a movie by yourself? It's great! You get to keep all of the popcorn to yourself because you don't have to share it. The best thing is that you get to choose any movie you want to see! Shop this way and you'll have even more fun. Remember, it's all about you Boo!

- **You'll be your own critic:** You can look at yourself in the mirror and decide if you feel good about what you're purchasing. If you don't like it, then you will put it back. You will have to be honest with yourself, but it's going to help you make better style choices. Even if you have to be blunt with yourself at first.

- **You will guide your shopping by what feels good to you:** Gone are the days when you and a shopping partner are looking for the latest things to wear.   You will begin to shop on your own and find things that feel good to you. And that might be your only shopping guideline.

- **You'll dress for you:** No longer are you dressing to impress your shopping partner. You can begin to shop and to buy things that impress you. Sure, you might show things to your friends, but only after you are confident with your choices.

- **This is where your instincts start to shout.** They will tell you what's best for you. Listen, and you will learn how to do this all over your life.

Now, this doesn't mean you shouldn't shop with others.

All this means is that when you're first starting to uncover your powerful style, you might want to focus more on yourself at first.

Take yourself out shopping more often than not, at first.

Get comfortable with the style you want to have. Once you are confident, then you will be able to shop with anyone, no matter what they have to say.

And it's going to really solidify what YOU want to wear.

You want to make sure that you are filling your closet with powerful clothes that make you feel good about who you are and about what you want to do in your life.

You don't want to fill your closet with clothes that caused a reaction for your shopping buddy.

While that's nice, you're the one who has to wear the clothes and the one who has wasted money on things that weren't the best for you.

What You Really Want To Wear

Of course, what DO you want to wear?

Everything looks so good on mannequins and websites, but what do you really want to wear?

It's time for a fashion show of sorts.

When you want to make sure that you feel good in what you wear, you need to look at what makes you feel good. And that isn't always what you think it should be.

Let me make this clearer.

All of us have outfits that make us feel amazing. AMAZING. We can put on that pantsuit or that dress and feel like a celebrity.

Even though we're not.

And while we might think that it's just a piece of clothing, it's not. It's special.

The piece of clothing is something that makes us feel special because it works with our body.

No matter what we might be doing that day and no matter what we might be thinking about, that outfit made us feel powerful.

We all have outfits like this.

Time to remember why they made us feel great.

- **Go through your closet:** Look at your closet again and see what you own. Put the clothing into piles of I LOVE IT and I DISLIKE IT. This will help you to see just how much further you have to go to create a wardrobe that you love.

- **Pull out your favorites:** Pull out everything that makes you feel amazing. They can be casual, formal, or just plain batty. It doesn't matter. What matters is that they make you feel great.

- **Try on your favorites:** Try them on, one by one. Stand in front of a mirror and look at them from the front and the back. You want to be able to see every inch of your body and what it looks like when you're dressed in things that make you smile.

- **Write about what works:** Look in the mirror and write down the things that you love about something. Look at the colors, the shapes, the lines, the details, etc. Write about all of the things that you absolutely LOVE about the outfit. You might also want to write down the things that make the outfit unique.

- **Write about how you feel:** Once you have those details down, then write down what you feel when you're wearing this outfit. Do you feel powerful? Skinny? Sexy? No answer is wrong. Just write about how you feel in the moment when you put on the outfit.

- **Notice brands and designer labels:** When you're ready to change into the next favorite outfit, take it off take notice of who the designers are. Keep a list of them because you will turn to them whenever you look for a new outfit.

- **Find similar looks:** Try to look online and in stores to find similar looks that have all of the details that you loved in the favorite outfits you tried on. This will help you have a better understanding of what you want to buy when it comes time to start buying new things.

- **Buy more than one of something you love:** If you find something that you LOVE, then why not buy more than one of it? This will help you to only have things you love in your closet and things that will make you happy. Buy multiple colors or the same color.

Once you've done this process with one outfit, continue on until you have tried on and evaluated all of your favorite outfits.

This process will give you a strong sense of your style in relation to what makes YOU happy and comfortable.

Imagine how much better your shopping trips will be once you start practicing this new information.

Forgetting Others

Yes, it's hard to forget what others have to say about the things we wear.

We might think of the ONE comment we get that's less than positive and by replaying it in our minds over and over. The human brain tends to remember the negative comments much more than it remembers positive ones. This is why remaining positive, and surrounding yourself with positive people is so important.

When you want to create power in your life in relation to your style, you need to focus ONLY on yourself.

This is not just a practice that will help you fill your closet with things that make you happy, it's also a practice that will help you focus more on what you love in your life, instead of wasting time and energy on negativity.

And this is going to help you in:

- Love
- Work
- Finances
- Family
- Children
- Life

You get the idea.

When you know what YOU want, you can communicate it to others.

You can speak up when you're not getting what you want.

You can stand up to people who ignore your needs.

Yes, your clothing choices and your ability to tune out everyone else is going to help you become a better person.

Not bad, huh?

Here are some ways you can begin to tune others out:

- **Ignore them:** Yes, you can just ignore what others say. You're the one who's wearing the clothes anyway.

- **Shop on your own:** No matter what you might think about shopping with a close friend, you need to start shopping on your own. And go shopping with friends, just don't buy anything unless you can be sure that you're making the choice on your own.

- **Speak up:** When someone else tells you that your style is _____, tell them to _____. Fill in the blank by speaking up for yourself and for the things that you want in your life. It's not always fun or easy, but it's something you should do for yourself. Eventually, people will get the hint.

- **Surround yourself with things you love:** No matter what you're wearing or what you're doing, try to surround yourself with things you love. You shouldn't ever feel like you're in a place that's not completely supportive of your happiness. Buy flowers for yourself, for example. The more you begin to think about what you want in your life, the more you will make choices that reflect what you truly want.

- **Start asking yourself what you want:** While this sounds silly, you might want to ask yourself what you want from life. Just the act of asking yourself what you want and what you don't want will inspire you to focus your thoughts in a positive and open direction. The more that you begin to think about how to answer these simple questions, the more you will make decisions with these ideas in mind, unconsciously.

- **Consider the motivations of others:** If someone says you look fat or you're frumpy, don't believe them. Stop and think about WHY they might be saying something. This will help you start listening to yourself instead of listening to others. Almost everyone has an agenda. Even your closest friends. Choose to be around supportive friends who want the best for you. Remember, we can't choose our family, but we sure can choose our friends. And heck, we can also choose to be around family even less – if they try to make us feel bad about ourselves. Life is all about choices. So is this book!

- **Remind yourself of how you feel when you wear what you like:** When you're still having troubles deciding whether to listen to someone else, remind yourself of what you feel like when you have what you want on your body. How YOU feel is ALL that matters.

- **Focus your energy in places that support what you want:** Let's dive back into something a bit deeper here. When you steer in one direction when you're driving, your car will follow the direction you take it. If you always listen to the negative people in your life or follow their advice, (chances are you feel down about yourself pretty often.) Stop it. Be with people who are positive who say things that are positive, and don't waste your time with anyone who wants to change you.

Your power is worth more.

You need to stand up for yourself.

You need to 'meet' yourself and your style by listening to what you say and what you think.

Everyone has an opinion, but yours is the ONLY one that matters.

By tuning out the naysayers, you can become your own person – powerful and strong.

Don't hold yourself back by someone else's limited beliefs for their own life.

You don't have to be held back because someone else thinks you 'should' do this or you 'should' do that.

You don't have to do anything that doesn't make you grin from ear to ear.

You don't.

Ever!

Step 4
Life Without A Mirror

Look at yourself - without looking at a mirror - right now.

Can you do it?

Close your eyes and try to see yourself as though you're looking in a full length mirror. What do you see when you first look at yourself?

- A crooked nose
- A wide waist
- A bright smile
- A sleek neck
- Possibilities?

We live in a world that seems to want perfection.

As though it were possible.

We live in a world where we can be digitally manipulated and altered to the precise specifications of science and the wide world of fashion.

We can change anything and make anything look BETTER.

So why not change ourselves?

Is it a good thing to constantly reach out to have more, to be more, and impress more?

Or are we wasting our time?

There are arguments in favor of each direction, to be sure. You might think that you can always be better, and that this helps you to prevent being dull or boring. Or that it helps you achieve and acquire more in life.

True.

But when you're reaching for an ideal of perfection, an ideal that does NOT exist, you may reach out and never really hold onto anything that resembles your true power.

Think about it.

When you stop reaching for perfection, you use your energy to do many more wonderful things that make you feel happier anyway.

You won't have to reach any further than yourself.

But you need to see yourself first.

Let's start looking at you.

What Do You See?

When you look in the mirror, stop looking at what you want to change.

Right now, get in front of a mirror and look at your face.

We'll start there, but we're going to move onto the rest of your body in a bit.

This is a process that is scary as can be, to be sure. No matter how beautiful you've been told you are, it's hard to see it.

Even when it's staring back at you.

Take a moment to look at the different parts of your face today.

- Your forehead
- Your eyes
- Your cheeks
- Your nose
- Your mouth
- Your chin

Looking around your face, look to see what is there.

This is not a process where you're going to write down everything you're doing, with plans to "fix" it. Put away that negative mental To Do List.

Right now, you're just looking.

You're looking at your face because it's something that you probably haven't really looked at for a while. Even if you prep in front of a mirror, you may not look to see what your entire face looks like.

Lovely.

Stop to look at your face and all of the things it DOES.

You can smile. You can cry. You can laugh. You can show anger.

All of these things can be expressed across your face. All of these things can be shown just from a look.

You can look at someone and make them look back.

You might be able to wink.

You might be able to smirk.

You might may funny faces.

All of these things happen because your face allows the message to go from your brain to your face muscles. You create what the world sees. If you're upset, you might keep things to yourself.

You pretend to be happy. You pretend to be calm.

All of this is what your face can DO.

You haven't thought of it that way before, have you?

All too often, we're too busy thinking about all of the things that we can't do or that we don't do.

And we forget that we are pretty darn amazing.

Now, stepping back from the mirror, look at the rest of your body.

Be nice now.

Look at your body and see what it does when you move your eyes over it. It's a good practice to start at a point on your head and then trace the outline of the body with your eyes.

What kind of shape are you?

What do you notice along the way?

Do you get stuck anywhere?

When you're looking at your body, push away any thoughts of judgment or disappointment.

This is not a time to think about how you want to change. This is a time to just appreciate what's there. You don't have to worry that you're doing anything wrong right now. You're not.

You're just looking at your body and seeing it.

Since you're doing this slowly and calmly, you might notice you aren't as upset by what you see. In fact, you may be sort of surprised at how beautiful you are.

You hadn't noticed all of the GOOD things about your body.

Now, that's what the mirror should be for. Seeing what's there, instead of what's not there or what you wish could be there.

Removing Life's Mirrors

Yes, you need to look in a mirror now and again.

You need to make sure that your spinach salad isn't stuck in your teeth and that your hair looks presentable before a meeting.

But the physical mirrors aren't the only ones that cause problems. There are other ways that you mirror the world's view of you.

And you must remove negative mirrors from your life, such as...

- Relying on the opinion of others.
- Others' negative opinions of you.
- Negative influences by the media.
- Clothing that doesn't flatter your body and your style.

When you listen to negative comments from others, whether they are warranted or not, you are looking at a mirror.

You will see what they see, not what is actually there.

Though you might not be able to stop the comments of everyone (though it would be nice, wouldn't it?), you can begin to selectively listen to what they say. You can create healthy boundaries around yourself so that you don't allow negativity into your life's mirror.

Listen to the things you want to remember, discard the rest.

The media, even though it is creative and expansive, also shows us images that are not realistic.

We look at models, think we're supposed to look like them, and then we're upset when we can't meet their unrealistic standards. Only one percent of all the women in the world are born with the type of body that has the measurements of a classic runway model.

Looking at ads in most magazines is like looking into a funhouse mirror –they always make you look bad. Unless you walk around with a professional air brush artist, Photo-shopper, and an army of stylists to do your hair, makeup and choose your clothing, it's impossible to reflect a magazine's images in your mirror. Even models can't do it without a team of experts. Believe me, I've seen many supermodels and celebrities in person. It "ain't" always that pretty.

Focus on looking at yourself, not others.

> Not models.
> Not celebrities.
> Not your friend with the best figure.

Focus on YOU.

This book is called *Stephany's Style Secrets; 7 Steps to Live and Dress YOUR Best*. It's not called 7 Steps to Dress Your Favorite Model's Best.

When you put on clothing that you own, you are already looking into a mirror of sorts. If you're holding onto clothing that's too loose or too tight, you're going to feel that you are larger than you are or that you are smaller than you want to be.

Choosing to wear clothing that fits is going to help you look into a truthful mirror.

A mirror that shows you a self that's actually there.

Some other ways to remove life's mirror include:

- **Always ask yourself what you think first:** This will give you a chance to hear what you have to say before others have a chance to butt in. While you might consider the opinions of others, what you think and what you feel is what matters before all else.

- **Avoid everyone and become a hermit:** Just kidding! ;)

You aren't going to be able to avoid all mirrors in life.

We still have to go out, we still need to head to the grocery store and we still need to talk to our families.

What can make these mirrors softer and more forgiving is having an attitude that you only see what you want to see – what you should see.

Which is exactly what you're doing right now anyway.

When you look in a mirror at yourself, you see one thing, but if someone else were to look into the mirror to see you, they would see something else.

Try this out with a close friend.

Ask them to look in a mirror and describe themselves while you stand behind them and describe what you see.

And then switch.

You might be surprised at what you hear because everyone thinks of themselves differently than others do.

Even if you think you're a completely objective person – you're not.

Start being positively subjective about your looks and about your life.

Why be negative when being positive is so much more enjoyable?

Looking At Your Reflection

When you look in the mirror, you might not always be happy.

But you still have to look.

Wait...this tip is about NOT looking in the mirror!

What I really want to tell you is that - there is a BETTER way of using the mirror in your life.

Stop looking at the mirror as an enemy or as a place where your mood drops and your smile disappears.

It doesn't have to be that way.

You can have all of the happiness you want, just from using the mirror in a new way.

Don't believe it? I understand that.

Try anyway.

Look at your reflection with a bit of a different take on what you see. What you DO see.

We're taught that looking in the mirror is the way to 'catch' our flaws before anyone else sees them.

Let's stop that sort of thinking, okay? We're forgetting our flaws now!

Instead, let's take a different approach when you look in the mirror:

- **Smile:** That's right, smile when you look at yourself in the mirror. Smiling helps you associate a good mood with the way you look, which is going to help you continue to look better and better. You'll get used to smiling when you think of your appearance, and you should.

- **Point out what's great:** Every day when you're in the mirror point out the things that are really looking good for you. For example, if you just got a full night's sleep, your skin probably looks AMAZING. Look at it, touch it, and enjoy how hot you look.

- **Compliment yourself:** Out loud, yes even if others are around, tell yourself how beautiful you are. Even if you feel like you should hide in your bedroom forever, stop the madness and tell yourself just how beautiful you think you are. Tell yourself again and again and again until you start to believe it.

- **Point out how great you look to others:** If you think you look good one day, then make sure others see it. Let others know that you're really happy that your _____ looks good. You don't have to be an egomaniac about it, but it never hurts to show off once in a while.

The mirror can be your friend. It wants to be your friend.

You don't have to be in a constant battle over what you see and what you think you see.

The truth is in the mirror.

But you've been lying to yourself before now. You've been looking in the mirror and saying that you don't look good.

That's a lie.

You do look good. But you've been focusing your attention on features of your body that might not be what you want them to be.

Instead, stop wasting your energy there and start using your energy to simply enjoy the beauty that is there.

Enjoy the way that you look right now.

There is always something to compliment and something to enjoy.

Other ways to make mirror time more enjoyable:

- **Tell yourself you love yourself:** This is probably not something you'll do right away. The first time I tried this I fell over laughing. It just seems silly. But when you think about it, if you can't tell yourself you love yourself, who will and why should they? I'll repeat it again...material possessions won't make you happy...and neither will someone who loves you. Feeling loved feels great, especially at first, but only YOU can love yourself unconditionally no matter what. Only YOU can make you happy.

- **Take your time:** When you look in the mirror, don't just focus on the parts of your body that you don't like. Notice parts of your body that are beautiful.

- **Don't look when you're stressed out:** If you're already feeling down about your life, why look in the mirror? You're only going to focus on those things you feel bad about since you're already in a bad mood. Instead...

- **Turn on a good song:** Remember your theme song? Find a way to make your mirror time fun and light. Spend some time finding a song that makes you feel like a rock star. And play it every time you look in the mirror. Play it until you can't get it out of your head.

Yes, your mirror can become your best friend.

Or at least, you can call a truce.

Stylish Confidence Boosters

Still not sure what to do when you look in the mirror?

Still think the mirror shows you what you don't want to see?

It's time to bring in some confidence reinforcements.

- **Affirmation time:** To make sure you're always focusing on the positive when you're in the mirror, create an affirmation you can refer to. Write words that remind you you're beautiful. Tape it on your mirror, and read it out loud every time you look at yourself. The more you do it, the more you will remind yourself to stay positive. Something as simple as 'You're amazing' will help you stay in the best frame of mind when you look in the mirror, and when step away.

- **Pretty up the mirror space:** Where is your mirror right now? The bathroom? Your bedroom? Make sure that the area around your mirror is tidy and pretty. When you look in the mirror, you want to focus on you, not on all of the mess that's strewn around the mirror or getting in your way when you look at yourself. Ideally, you should buy, build or create a vanity, like the kind that women used during the art deco era in the 1920s. When a woman at that time got dressed, she started by sitting down on a beautiful satin covered stool (known as a "poof"), in front of a detailed little table called a "vanity" that had a very large mirror in front of it. She powdered her nose, applied her makeup and sprayed her perfume with beautiful containers made of hand made silver or glass. Whether you go that far or not, I hope this gave you a picture of the kind of experience I want you to have when you look in the mirror. Honey, it's all about spoiling yourself with the best you can afford, even if it only lasts 10 minutes a day.

- **Wear only what you want:** It's true, the more you wear clothing that you love, the more confident you will be. Be completely who you are in terms of your style. Enjoy it.

- **Add a pretty piece of jewelry:** A good way to remind yourself of what you really look like and what you have to offer in the world is by wearing a sentimental piece of jewelry that you love. Wear it every single day. Every time you see it, remind yourself that you are beautiful, inside and out.

- **Ask for compliments:** If you have been having troubles with your personal power for a while, it's never a bad idea to enlist help along the way. Talk to your friends about simply giving you compliments whenever possible. In time, you will be able to compliment yourself. And you'll be able to recognize the friends who appreciate you the most because showering you with compliments will be easy for them to do once you ask.

- **Post pictures of yourself in your happiest times:** Have you ever noticed that when you're really happy and someone takes your picture that you photograph so much better? It was because you were relaxed, having fun, and you were probably not thinking about what you looked like. Post the pictures around your house and your mirror, to remind yourself of how lovely you are when you're happy and confident.

Confidence is something you can wear, and you can accessorize it with happiness.

While this concept might not seem to fit at first, keep trying it on until you feel it settle over your skin and into your mind.

Know That You Look GREAT

The mirror tells you something every time you use it.

But the mirror doesn't have to be your judge. You shouldn't rely on it to determine whether you're going to feel good or bad about your day.

Just like the scale shouldn't have power over you either.

Here are some ways to take back YOUR feeling of looking great.

- **Tell yourself you look good:** Before you walk out the door, make sure to tell yourself that you look good. This will set the tone for your day. Before you walk into a room, or a meeting, or enter an event, repeat the affirmation you posted on your mirror "You're amazing!" Repeat it again and again throughout the day.

- **Make an effort to look great:** Of course, before you leave, you need to make an effort to look good. Every time you dress well and you dress to impress yourself, the more confident you will feel – with and without a mirror.

- **Laugh more:** When you allow yourself to laugh, you can focus on the feeling that everything is okay and that all of this style talk isn't serious anyway. Try to find more humor in your life by watching more funny shows or just being with people who make you laugh. Hard. I'm going against many of my colleagues' opinions in the fashion industry by saying what I'm about to say...fashion is NOT rocket science! It ain't that deep! What IS deep is how you feel about yourself, and how you can USE fashion and your personal style to elevate your self-esteem.

- **Make a list of things that you love about yourself:** Really, you can't do this one enough. Read it until you have it memorized. Repeat it as a mantra during your affirmations.

- **Forget the mirror:** After you've looked in the mirror, stop looking. You don't need to pour over yourself for the rest of the day. Stop to see if your teeth are clean after lunch, then stop obsessing. Refresh your hair, check your makeup and move on.

The mirror can become your friend.

But even your best friends don't need to see you every single second of the day.

Instead, focus on your life – that's what matters.

The mirror will still be there later.

This is life without a mirror.

Step 5

Discover Your Personal Style

Either you have style, or you don't — right?

Not quite.

Style is about more than clothes.

Style is...

- What sets you apart.
- What makes you feel like yourself.
- Being comfortable in your own skin.
- The way you live your life.
- The way you treat others.
- The way you treat yourself.
- The way you project confidence in yourself.
- The way you carry yourself.

Have you ever met someone who could wear a sack and they always look great no matter what? Their style has more to do with how they carry themselves, how they feel about themselves, and how they walk through life, than the clothes on their back.

Style is not just about clothing. But it can certainly be enhanced by clothes you wear. At the same time, when you rely too much on clothing or trends, you might set yourself up for negative feelings if you choose the 'wrong' thing.

(More on that later.)

If you've looked in your closet more than once and thought you had nothing to wear, that's definitely not the case. Instead, you may not have the pieces you need to create a style that makes you feel gorgeous.

Let's examine what makes your style tick, even if you never find a name for it.

What Is Style Anyway?

Style is an indescribable state of being for most people.

It's that special thing that makes heads turn or makes someone stand out in a crowd.

Style is something everyone wants, no one is sure they have, and very few know how to get.

Style is...

- An expression of who you are.
- An expression of how you feel.
- The way you dress.
- The way you shop.
- The way you want to be identified.

Style is about the way that you want to feel in the world and the way you want to be seen.

When creating your personal style, be careful not to choose things that aren't absolutely perfectly who YOU are.

You don't want to go out, buy a bunch of clothes and then come home and not recognize the person who's supposed to be wearing them.

Style occurs when you put on an outfit and you think to yourself – *hey, that looks like me.*

As a result, style is difficult to define because everyone is different.

Style is about expressing who you really are, which can be quite scary. You want people to like the person you think you are – that's why wearing certain clothes is called a fashion RISK.

Find a style that makes you feel so confident that you don't care what others think.

That's personal power and personal style tied up in chic a bow!

Borrowing From Other Styles

Now you've looked at, tried on and maybe purchased various styles in stores. You've flipped through lots of your favorite magazines, you've searched fashionable websites, and you've consulted with your most positive and supportive friends.

But does this mean that you know what your style is? No.

What you want to do is to think about the styles that are already available to you and pick out the best parts of them. Does this mean that everything is going to work together?

Probably not. But that's not the point right now.

The goal right now is to find out what styles are out there and what you enjoy from each of them.

If you don't enjoy one style in its entirety, then that's fine too.

What you need to know right now is that other styles are waiting to be borrowed from.

That's the point of fashion – to grab what's already out there, make it new by making it your own.

(Here's another Stephany Style Secret: NOTHING in fashion is really new. Everything is just redesigned, restyled, reshaped and reformed into something that seems new. Millions of clothing lines and fashion magazines are sold with this notion every day. But if your eye isn't trained to see this, you'll never notice it, and you'll fall for it by buying the "latest trends" every season.)

A few of the types of styles you may choose to reflect might include:

- Classic
- Modern
- Avant Garde
- Urban Chic
- Lolita
- Bohemian
- Diva
- Metrosexual
- Glamour Goddess

This is a very short list because it can be divided and subdivided into even more categories.

What you call your style isn't actually all that important.

It's how you wear your style that matters when you're out in the world.

You need to figure out what you want to wear, how you want to wear it and what it means for your closet.

And your shopping list.

Let's think about what your style might be for a minute. If someone were to ask you what your personal style is (ideally), what would you say?

How would you describe what you're wearing if you were on the phone?

If you could only use words, and no pictures, how would you describe your style?

Think about these words:

- Loose, billowy, flowy styles
- Form fitting
- Utilitarian
- Professional
- Eclectic
- Nonconforming

You get the idea.

You can certainly come up with more descriptors than that. But the more words you use to describe what you want to look like, the easier it will be to find and name your style.

Start by writing down all of the words you associate with your style, or the new style you are trying to achieve.

Take the list on your next shopping trip, and ask yourself if the items you are buying match the list of descriptors in your hand.

If not, don't buy it.

If so, buy it and enjoy what you've purchased.

If the idea of naming your style doesn't appeal to you, that's okay too – there's no judgment here.

Narrowing down what you will and will not wear is just as effective and just as fun to do.

A Style Mentor?

Some people may find it easier to copy the style of someone else when they're first learning about fashion and dressing for power.

Nothing is wrong with this.

The only reason why we're not focusing on this more is that when you emulate someone else, you will tend to purchase clothing to keep up with their style, instead of yours.

This can be costly in more ways than one.

But if you're interested in finding out if a certain fashion mentor's style is for you (and your checkbook doesn't mind), try to wear things you've seen on them. Imitation is (supposedly) the sincerest form of flattery.

The more that you imitate, the more you will find out if someone else's style is right for you. Although you may shop at the same stores as they do, try to buy things that are more you than "them."

And while you may love the way they dress, you might find that their style isn't right for your body type.

At the same time, you might find style mentors in other arenas outside of the fashion world:

- **Personal shoppers:** You might not think of a personal shopper as a style mentor. Think again. If you see a sales person or personal shopper whose style you like, adopt them as your favorite salesperson whenever you shop there. They can help you customize their style to yours, by finding clothing in the same store to flatter your body type.

- **Celebrities:** Many people are inspired and influenced the most by celebrities. But their outfits can come at quite a high price. Instead of focusing on WHAT they're wearing, think about HOW they are wearing it.

Ideally, you should be your own style mentor.

As I said before, you should listen to your own affirmations, study your list of favored styles, dress to flatter your figure, and follow your own instincts.

But if none of the above makes you comfortable, it doesn't hurt to emulate others for guidance.

Once you begin to get a sense of what works for you, then it's time to tinker with the style you've chosen.

And make it your own.

Changing Your Personal Style

Maybe you're afraid of change because you've always dressed in a particular way, and changing would break you out of your comfort zone.

This makes sense.

You want to stick with what you know.

There's no reason why you can't stick with what you know and make it even better.

Truthfully, it doesn't matter what you wear. It's more about HOW you wear it.

Think of a celebrity's style you admire. When you see them in pictures, you're not looking at the clothing they wear.

Really, you're not.

Instead, you're looking at the way they look. And they look pretty amazing. Don't forget that most of them hire professional stylists to dress them whenever they're appearing before paparazzi.

Instead of focusing on paparazzi proof celebrity style, focus on capturing something in your style that allows you to look good, no matter what you wear. You've learned about how to become more confident, but now it's time to take those lessons and wear them on your sleeve.

Literally.

Here are some tips for changing your personal style:

- **Start small:** If you're a little nervous about trying something new, try out something small. Adding something as small as a new necklace or an old hat will help you stand out more and it will help you see that your small fashion choices are adding up to big results to others around you.

- **Clean up:** It's always a great money saver to take extra time to care for the clothing you already have. Getting it tailored to fit better, dry cleaning more frequently, and ironing it well, can impact your personal style, even if you decide not to buy anything new.

- **Dress up:** Get a little more dressed up for work tomorrow and enjoy your co-workers' compliments all day long. Just taking the time to carefully select an outfit will help you wade into the waters of a new personal style.

- **Start on weekends:** If you're still nervous about trying out a new look, do so on the weekend. Walk around town in your new outfit and watch your neighbors' reactions. Actually, it's going to be better to see what your own reaction is since you're the one who's wearing it. See how YOU feel when you're getting your groceries dressed to the nines!

- **Have a fashion show:** Stage your own personal fashion show at home. Create stylish looks and model them up and down your hallway. If you like a certain look, take a picture of it so you can remember how to put it together again.

- **Focus less on style and more on how you feel:** In the end, it's really, really not about the clothing you wear, it's about how you feel wearing it.

If you're not comfortable with what you're wearing, change it.

If you try a new style that makes you feel odd, don't wear it again.

If you find a style that makes you feel AMAZING, buy it in every color.

Creating your style is a process of slowly incorporating more pieces into your wardrobe that make sense to you.

When you try something new, you'll want to try more.

And, over time, your personal style will develop.

Unless you hire a personal stylist to do this work for you, you'll end up doing it for yourself.

Don't worry, YOU have all the tools you need!

Creating A Trademark Look

When you want to stand out more than you already do for your personal style, find ONE THING that makes you, you.

Most people won't remember what you wore last week.

What they will remember is the statement making piece you wore that no one else had.

They'll remember the thing that made you stand out in the crowd.

A fun way to create your trademark look is to start with just one accessory that you wear every single day – no matter what. When you wear a signature piece, it makes you unique.

Some ideas for signature pieces include:

- A bright scarf.
- A gigantic necklace.
- A wide brim hat (in the appropriate setting).
- Chunky earrings.
- A large watch.
- A wrap with a recognizable print – Pucci, Burberry, leopard, zebra, etc.
- A striking hair color or hair cut.

Each of these items is easy to put on and off, and they can coordinate with almost any outfit.

When you wear them every day, you link a lot of your outfits together.

Even if you don't the piece when you're at work (though you should try), you can create something that people will use to recognize you when you're at an event...like a celebrity who's known for their hair.

What would the Editor in Chief of Vogue Magazine, Anna Wintour, be without her enormous black sunglasses and perfect black bob haircut?

What would Cher be without her sleek black hair?

What would Karl Lagerfeld be without his dark sunglasses and personal fan?

What would Brad Pitt be without his eternally perfect 5 o'clock shadow?

These are details that set them apart from the rest.

Your Style Will Evolve Over Time

Every day, make choices to try new things, test out new outfits, and take new risks.

Over time, you will decide what works best for you.

And what doesn't.

No matter what you do, enjoy the results because you're focusing your attention on how you feel.

You deserve the extra attention.

Step 6
Risks Equal Rewards

When we met at the beginning of this book, I mentioned that I had taken a humungous risk in my life ten years ago. I CHOSE to go from making over $100,000 a year as a fashion designer in New York, to making $3.50 an hour as a waitress in Miami. I did it because I wanted – NEEDED – to find happiness in myself, outside of my friends, my love life, my family, my career, and my stress-filled life that were affecting my health. I had to let go of caring about what other people thought of me. I suffered through hearing how 'crazy' some of them thought I was. I let go of some THOSE PEOPLE too. And guess what...in the process of literally losing people who weren't the best for me, I simultaneously lost the 10 pounds that refused to come off before!

By taking a risk I realized...I take myself with me wherever I go. I realized I didn't have to look for happiness outside myself. It existed in me all along. I just had to discover it. And, for a while, I was happier making $3.50 an hour than I ever was as an overly stressed out fashion executive making $100,000 a year. I had found peace in being me.

I am not saying I haven't struggled with this concept since then. I do. It's just that when I gave up everything – I gained everything. And 10 years later, I continue to tap into that feeling almost every day.

I know the risks I speak of in this chapter, and in this book because I've lived, survived and thrived through them myself. But, let's move on, because the rest of this story is in my next book.

Now, back to you!

Fashion can be risky. But risks are exciting. They get the blood pumping and they allow you to bring something new and energetic in your life.

When you take a risk, there's always the chance that you might not succeed. You might try on an outfit, think it's amazing, wear it and realize it wasn't perfect for an event, it was too uncomfortable, or it simply didn't flatter you enough.

But if you like it, then it doesn't really matter does it? If only it were that easy.

Try new looks that make you feel great, even if the rest of the world shakes its head at you.

Fashion is about risk — this can't be repeated enough.

For those who are afraid to take risks, it's time to be bold.

Fashion Faux Pas?

What does the idea of a fashion mistake, a fashion misstep, and a fashion faux pas really mean?

Um, nothing.

Really. Think about it for one minute. If you were a mother and someone said you were raising your child the wrong way, what would you do?

Smack them, probably.

But when you're told that your outfit isn't as stylish as it could be, you just simply accept it.

NO MORE!

People are going to say what they're going to say. And there's really nothing you can do except ignore them.

The only fashion faux pas you need to worry about are:

- Clothing that is dirty.
- Clothing that is wrinkled (and it's not meant to be).
- Clothing that is ill-fitting, and reveals bulges, etc

Outside of these no-no's, you're golden.

The truth is that there are always going to be people who don't agree with the way you dress.

When it comes down to creating power in your life with your style, there's nothing wrong with the way that you dress. Ever.

When you like what you're wearing, it is clean, pressed, and fits you well, that's really all that matters when you walk out the door. Now, if you're not happy with what you're wearing, then you probably should choose something else.

But if you're happy, the rest of the world's criticisms should go in one of your ears and out the other.

Risks And Fashion

It may take a certain amount of risk to develop the look you want.

What do you want to achieve, and how are you going to get it?

Here are some questions to contemplate right now:

- What fashion trends are weird to you?
- What do you consider risky?
- What would you NEVER wear?
- What do you think is risky when other people wear it?

Now...TRY ONE OF THESE RISKS!

You might absolutely hate what you're doing. And if you can't see yourself walking out the door in a risk, then you don't have to.

Trying something that's absolutely scary and terrifying demonstrates your inner power, no matter what you wear.

Taking a risk from time to time, wearing something that you think is a little frightening, is a great way to remind yourself that you are a powerful woman.

Risks are healthy, after all.

While you might not want to take risks when you're at work or when you're in certain situations, it's a good idea to have at least one thing in your closet that is risky.

Whether this means you have a wild print or texture, or a pair of sky high shoes, try wearing them with other things that make you feel comfortable.

Eventually what's risky today won't feel risky at all tomorrow.

Now you can EXPAND your life as well as your fashion choices.

Risks = rewards.

Celebrities are slammed for the fashion choices they make – and don't make.

Follow your own inner celebrity by experiencing the rewards of taking risks:

- **Broader fashion style:** When you don't restrict yourself to the 'fun' stuff, your closet will have far more possibilities than you thought you could have before.

- **Others want to copy you:** Yes, when you are a trendsetter, others will follow you, even if they think you're crazy for starting the trend in the first place.

- **People feel comfortable around you:** If you're a person who creates their own fashion trends, you'll be even more interesting as a human being.

- **You can wear ANYTHING:** That's right, when you're bold and you're risky, it doesn't matter what you wear. You have no limits on what you can wear.

Others in your life will follow your lead – even if they say that you're a big fashion faux pas, at first.

Some of today's best known styles started out as a designer's bad idea.

And they eventually caught fire in popularity. Just like you can, and will.

How To Take Risks The Right Way

Taking risks can cause negative reactions in one way or another.

There is no right or wrong way of taking a risk.

If you're the type of person who prefers rules before starting on anything, find the best ways to take the risks you want to take.

Here are some ideas for making sure that you take the risks you want, with the best intentions.

- **Do it boldly:** Heck, if you're going to take a fashion risk, it might as well be something that is so bold that it can't be ignored. Go big or go home, right?

- **Do it with friends:** When you're ready to take some fashion risks, it's a great idea to do it first with friends and then with people you don't know. They will give you feedback (you can't stop it anyway), but their feedback will sting far less than hearing it from strangers.

- **Do it with an announcement:** If you show up in a bold outfit you know will make people wonder what you're thinking, tell them what you're thinking. When you state the obvious, no one can turn away. And you take proactive initiative in your life head on.

- **Try something new a few different ways:** If you have something risky in your closet that you never thought you'd wear, add it to accentuate your look gradually, and just change up the way that you wear other things. For example, if you have a leopard print scarf, try it first as a scarf, then as a belt, then as a headband, etc. You will find one that works best for you.

- **Figure out what you are afraid of:** Think about why you're so afraid when it comes to taking fashion risks. If it's that you think others will judge your weight or your style, then challenge this assumption in your head. Boldly do something that scares you and then see whether there was anything to be afraid of in the first place. Probably not. Fear is ALL in our minds. Did you know that it doesn't exist? No one MAKES us fearful. We do it to ourselves, and most of the time when it comes to fashion, fears are based on caring about other people's opinions more than our own.

- **Challenge your closet to find new looks:** Find ways to rearrange the outfits you already have. Mix things up and see what you can come up with. This is very low on the list in the degree of risk, since it's using clothes you already wear. But with a new arrangement, your wardrobe will be bolder and more exciting. There are things in your closet right now that are dying to be worn together. They might seem crazy, but if you create a look that turns heads, chances are great that you'll get more compliments than criticisms.

- **Stay away from the little black dress:** We all have one dress we feel good in and turn to when we want to make sure we look great. However, when you stick to just one outfit every time you go out, you're not being risky. You're playing it safe. There's nothing wrong with this, but when you want to develop your own style by pushing past your safety zone, you have to do something different to shake things up a bit.

- **Pull together one new look a week:** Every week, find a new outfit to wear in your closet. If you tend to wear the same lineup of outfits each week, change things up to figure out what risks you're willing to take.

Think about the last time you dressed up for Halloween.

You probably, no, most definitely, wore something that was a bit risqué and certainly not your style.

Why?

Because it was a holiday? Maybe so. You also wore something new and fun because you felt comfortable to take a risk.

With the excuse of it being Halloween, you were able to take that risk and not worry as much about what others thought, especially because everyone, including kids and adults, were also in costumes. You were just dressing up.

When you look at each day as though it's a chance to be risqué (however you define it), you will be able to look at fashion as something that's fun to use in your life.

Instead of locking yourself into what's right or wrong.

Fun is the name of the game with style and with fashion.

And it shouldn't be a secret any longer.

A lot of people talk about intelligent risk taking – you can follow this approach too.

There are steps you can take to ensure that your risks are carefully thought out and planned.

And while that doesn't seem spontaneous – and it's not – it might just be what you do until you can take more risks with your riskiness.

- **Do your research:** When you're first thinking about taking risks (not only with fashion, but also in your life), it helps to do your research. Find out not only what others consider to be risky, but also what you consider to be risky.

- **Know what the results might be:** Close your eyes and think about what might happen when you wear something that isn't normal. Are bad things really going to happen? Nope.

- **Don't give up:** Even if no one is responding or you're not feeling powerful about it, keep taking risks. This will help you create a comfort with risk taking, and eventually you will get over your fears.

- **Reward yourself:** When you do something risky, make sure that you reward yourself for it. This is a great step and one you should acknowledge yourself for by taking notice of it.

- **Celebrate your successes:** Did taking a risk go well? Have someone take a picture of this risky outfit and post the picture somewhere that anyone can see it.

- **Know your limits:** Of course, you might have to limit your risks when you're in certain environments. Make sure you know your limits before you begin to take your risks. Nothing's worth getting arrested ;).

In time, you'll do all of this naturally.

And you'll love it.

Risk = Power

When you take risks with your style, you make yourself vulnerable.

If you've been feeling like you're less than powerful in your life, the idea of taking risks probably seems, well, risky. Uncomfortable.

But with each risk you take, you also take a step in the direction of empowering yourself. With each outfit you wear that doesn't seem to add up when compared to fashion magazines, you are setting forth on a new adventure.

And no one has to follow you, because it's all about you, Boo.

The power that comes along with risk taking is something most people don't realize. Oh, we might realize it if we do something bold and we feel AMAZING afterward.

But that feeling dissipates, just as every feeling does.

Taking risks is good for the soul, though most of us would rather protect the status quo than dive into the unknown.

(But what if all of the happiness you ever wanted exists in the unknown?)

When you take a risk, you get to enjoy tremendous benefits, such as...

- **Discovering your power:** When you switch the energy of your style, you switch the energy of who you are. The more you try out new styles, the closer you get to aligning your style with who you really are. And that is power.

- **You will feel confident:** When you wear something that makes you feel amazing, you feel confident. If you always feel like you look amazing, then you will ALWAYS be confident.

- **You will focus more on others:** If you're confident in yourself, you focus less on yourself and more on giving to those around you. This empowers your personal interactions and it honors yourself worth for "doing the right thing."

- **You will enjoy compliments:** Risk takers get more compliments than others, even if people don't like the risks they've taken. You'll get complimented on who you are and as someone who doesn't have to follow trends.

- **You will get noticed:** You already know this, but the risks you take lead you to get noticed. More opportunities will knock at your door because it's well known that those who take risks in one area of their lives are probably taking risks in other parts of their lives as well. Plus, it's a fantastic asset for your career.

- **You will be happier:** People who are confident enough to take risks are happier. When you're not constantly thinking about what you should be doing, you focus on what you ARE doing.

Risky behavior doesn't have to be dangerous in order to create a good feeling in your body and in your mind. What if you're someone who wears tons of tattoos, body piercings, or twelve-inch high spiked hair? (Even in your case,) most of the time, people who dress in the extreme only hang out with people who dress the way they do. This means they also live inside their comfort zone. Sometimes (NOT all the time), their desire to do drastic things to their bodies or wardrobes is based on needing to shock the public for attention rather than feeling truly confident and comfortable in their own skin.

Whether you choose to wear fifty piercings, practice body modification, or you truly happen to love avant garde punk style, wear it for the right reasons. If you look shocking, but all of your friends do too, maybe you should ask yourself why you only associate with friends who dress like you do. Could it be that you feel more comfortable with people who are like you? Could it be that you use shocking clothing to attract attention you should actually be giving to yourself? Release your fear! Let go and risk being different, while being comfortable with who you really are.

If your outer clothing is already risky, as yourself why. What would happen if you risked it all by dressing more conservatively? Would your friends alienate you because you no longer dressed the way they do? Would they tease you? Are they your real friends?

Whether you lean toward being extremely liberal or radically conservative, choose your style because it reflects who YOU are, not who your friends want you to be. Choose it because you are confident in knowing you are being yourself, without depending on the public.

When you take risks with your clothing in any capacity, you're showing that your inner world is also ready to take bold new risks too.

One step at a time, your life changes.

One outfit at a time, your perspective changes.

Everything changes.

The Truth About Others

Most of the time, images of other people just float in and out of our minds, and we don't give them a second thought.

Why not?

Well, have you noticed that your brain is filled with millions of other ideas at any given moment? Whether you're focusing on school, your family, or your career, your brain is often not 'there' when you're out in the world.

You're looking at your To Do list, and while you might notice someone's outfit, you may not remember it.

Unless it's very risky, or very striking.

Think about it for a minute.

Does clothing really impact anyone else? It might, momentarily, or it might impact those who are making clothing and who are looking for inspiration.

But does it really matter?

I hate to say it, but not really. Clothing and style only matter to the person who are wearing them – and that's really all that should matter.

It's when we start obsessing about whether anyone cares about what we look like, that we LOSE the power we want so badly.

It's when we give all of our power over to everyone else that we begin to get nervous.

- They won't like me if...
- They won't listen to me when...
- They won't think I'm a good person if...

Think about it. When you walk down the street today, try to remember everyone you saw. You can't do it without a photographic memory.

What I do remember is the feeling I had when I was walking down the street. I either felt confident and powerful, or I felt like I should have spent five more minutes on my hair – or worn a darn hat.

Because I wanted to look good for me.

Yes, I like to look put-together and I like to make sure that I'm not trailing a piece of toilet paper behind me (which has happened three times in my life!), but while that's the case, I don't have to stop and worry about everyone.

I have better things to do, and so do you.

No one else worries about you, so you shouldn't have to worry about yourself. All you need to worry about – if you really need something to worry about – is whether you feel good in what you're wearing.

Everything else is just a distraction.

Here's what you can do to forget about everyone else:

- **Don't comment on what others are wearing:** When you stop the cycle of commenting on what others are wearing, you can begin to focus on yourself and not others.

- **Look at yourself and focus on your look:** When it comes to your power, it's time to be selfish. While you might be a good person who wants to help and support others, you should only focus on what you look like and care about your style. Keep your mindset on what your power means to you and what you have to do to keep it.

- **Look in the mirror, once:** When you get ready in the morning, use a mirror. But don't keep looking in the mirror every hour to see if you STILL look good. Let it go.

- **Listen to what people say:** When talking with others, focus on what they are saying, not what they look like. Think about what they are projecting when they are with you. This means you should see who they are, not what they look like. Are they excited about a certain subject? Are they confident? Learn about these things and you will find out what they have that you might want to emulate, not their clothing.

- **Stop and think about how you feel:** You need to check in with yourself more often than you are right now. By thinking about how you feel in your clothing and in your life, you'll start changing the way that you interact with others and those that are in your world.

- **Tell yourself that you are confident and powerful:**, remind yourself over and over again that you are confident and powerful.

- **Remind yourself that you care about your style because you care about your power:** Your power is what matters. Styles change; opinions change, but how you feel about who you are doesn't have to.

The power that you have does not come from anyone else but you.

Nor should it.

When you can focus on yourself and on your power, the risks you take only enhance that power.

Think of this as testing how strong you can be.

You will find you're a lot stronger and more powerful than you've given yourself credit for.

What a terrific discovery.

This section has been about taking risks. By just picking up this book, you took a risk.

As you've been reading this book, maybe you've decided that everything you were doing was wrong.

Or, you could have already known a lot of the information in this book, and you don't agree with any of it.

Or, maybe you were introduced to some new concepts, and some that were not so new.

Either way, purchasing and reading a new book was a risk.

Don't you feel better for it in one way or another?

Risks are a good thing and something to treasure.

So, here are some final ways to get riskier:

- **Try one new thing a day:** Each day, try to do one new thing that you've never done before. While you might think of this as being impossible, there are a lot of little things that you have never tried before. Start by trying a food you've never eaten.

- **Take a new route to work:** Simply changing up the route you take to work can shake up your perspective and allow you to feel riskier and more confident in your life.

- **Talk to one new person every day:** If you're a person who likes to keep to yourself, find a new attitude. By taking time each day to introduce yourself to a stranger, you will be more powerful than you were the day before.

- **Schedule yourself for one impossible idea a year:** Have you wanted to climb a mountain? Swim in a bikini? Run a marathon? Travel to Europe? Each year, schedule yourself to accomplish at least one 'seemingly' impossible thing. You will discover that there are NO limits to what you can do.

You really don't have any limits - outside of the ones you impose on your own mind.

Get risky.

...And watch everything you'll do!

Step 7

You Look Great, Dammit!

Sometimes, you just need a cheerleader in life.

Even if you have everything you've ever wanted and everything is going perfectly, you should associate yourself with loving people to tell you that...

You're the best person ever.

You're the most stylish.

You're the most beautiful.

You're the fairest one of all, and

You look great, dammit!

✧ ✧ ✧

Oprah has Gayle.

Jennifer has Courtney.

Kate has Victoria.

✧ ✧ ✧

You get the idea. No matter who you are, you need someone to tell you that you're fabulous as often as possible.

Simply because you are.

I wrote this chapter for you to return to it again and again, whenever you need a pick-me-up, or a little hug.

Sometimes, you won't feel as great as they say you are, and while that's normal, it doesn't mean you have to settle for being blah.

You can be stunningly amazing in every moment. By building your confidence in who you are and what you look like, you can be perfectly perfect every moment.

Just keep reading the rest of this chapter if you're having one of those days/weeks/months where you disagree with how fabulous you are.

(Shh, we all have them.)

Looking In That Mirror

Right now, get in front of your mirror and take a good long look.

What do you see now? While maybe you have been hesitant to look before, things have probably changed. You're a different person than you were before you started this journey.

And you're ready to reach out and grab life instead of just waiting for it to happen to you.

That's what your inner power is.

When you have power, it's like having a full tank of gas everywhere to go. You can head out on the road of your life and see the sights instead of worrying about what kind of car you have.

Today, look in the mirror and appreciate all that you have done and all that you have changed in your mind.

You've done a lot of hard work and it has not always been easy to do. Sometimes, you thought I was full of bull and that I had it easy because I've already been confident in myself.

Can I tell you a secret? It wasn't always that way.

Once upon a time, I relied on the opinion of others when it came to making most of the decisions in my life. I called my girlfriends to ask them about every new guy I met. I asked them about everything that occurred in my love life, and I constantly compared their opinions before forming my own. Despite what my family may think, I carried their opinions in the back of my mind at all times.

As I mentioned in Chapter Six, I took drastic measures to change my life. By taking a huge risk, I eventually learned to trust, and therefore love myself, no matter what anyone else thought. I didn't know anyone when I relocated from New York to Miami. But for the first time in my life, I loved going to the movies by myself, I preferred going to the beach alone, I reveled in eating at cafes while reading my favorite magazines – all by myself. I loved my own company, and in turn, I learned to appreciate my own opinions more than ever before. I didn't have to ask anyone else how I should live my life. I learned how to listen to my own instincts to live my best life. I realized I didn't need a mirror to tell me I looked great. I didn't need a man to tell me I was beautiful. And I didn't need to rely on anyone else's opinion to live the life I was placed on earth for.

✧ ✧ ✧

I suspended my disbelief that I was anything less than absolutely perfect.

I stopped worrying about what I looked like.

One day it hit me – the only person standing in the way of all the things I wanted in my life was, ME! I was the one to blame for my unhappiness.

Not everyone else.

Keepin' it real. While everyone else might have an IMPACT on how you feel about yourself, they're not the ones in charge of what you feel. The only person who is in charge of what you feel and what you do is YOU.

When you start looking in the mirror and decide for yourself how you look, you can begin to stop worrying about what everyone else thinks and you can begin to live.

Truly live.

Right now, look in the mirror and tell yourself these four things:

- You're amazing.
- You're beautiful.
- You're successful.
- You're happy.

Simple, right? Powerful? Yes.

When you tell yourself things that are already true, your brain knows it, your heart knows it, and your life begins to realize it too.

When you can focus on the things you are starting to believe, you will see your life start to settle around you the way you've always wanted it to.

By simply believing in yourself, you can grab onto your power and finally take it for a ride.

Not the other way around.

When you are ready to look in the mirror and see EVERYTHING – and still love it – you are ready to launch the new you into the world. And the world will be ready to witness all that you have to say and all that you have to offer.

Let's talk about the mirror. You look at it and tell yourself what you've learned here, but what do you actually see?

Are you continuing to see flaws? Or are you allowing yourself to open up to the possibility that there's more to you than just things to be changed?

What do you SEE?

Take a moment to write down what you see, or to talk to yourself out loud.

When you're done, think hard about how you can make yourself even stronger. Carry these thoughts with you as reminders of what you want from the world and of how you will be seen in the world.

Notice I said how you WILL be seen, not how you want to be seen.

All this time, we've been talking about what you want from your life, but while that's positive, that also makes it sound like you're forever going to be reaching out for other things.

You don't have to reach out anymore.

You can hold onto what you want from your life. You create concrete results that were once mere dreams in your head.

Let's talk about your mind right now – and how to charge it up for positive power no matter what happens in your life.

You need a spa day for your brain:

- Clear out your thoughts.
- Come up with new affirmations.
- Do what you love.

To make sure you know what I'm talking about, let's go into more detail than this list.

You might think of your brain as being a great place to store information, much like your closet is a great place to store clothes.

But when you have too much noise, too many thoughts (and too many clothes), you can't find what you really need.

You can get lost in your own brain when you don't take the time to clean things up in there. And while you might have better intentions, you might find yourself reaching for the old thoughts that are closer to the front. This is the old comfort level that was mentioned earlier.

It's time to clean house.

You can clean up your thoughts by:

- **Quick meditation:** When you have too many thoughts in your mind, you need to find a way to settle and calm it down. You do this by exercising your brain and strengthening its quiet muscles. Meditation is a way to relax and clear your mind. You don't have to sit in a lotus position forever either. All you need to do is to spend ten minutes per day in a quiet place. Don't spend your time thinking about anything else. Just listen to your breathing or to a CD that has instrumental music. Practice it every day and you'll find it's easier to tell your brain to shut out negative thoughts as soon as they arise. And, eventually they will disappear.

- **Journaling:** You might be a person who is driven to write about things when you're upset, or when you have negative thoughts. Some believe that writing as much as you can first thing in the morning is a good way to clear out the brain before it has time to impact your day. But do what feels good to you. Release all of your noise on the paper, and you'll clear your mind of the things that don't help you.

- **Talking it out:** Express yourself out loud in a constructive manner. Consult with a close friend, someone you trust, and expel those empty good-for-nothing thoughts.

Next, since you've been doing so much changing, it's time you changed your life affirmations and created them into a mantra to repeat to yourself over and over again.

You need to start telling yourself new, fresh, and bold statements. In addition to 'I'm amazing,' you might want to include affirmations such as:

- I'm strong.
- I'm unstoppable.
- I'm powerful.
- I can do anything.

This is very powerful, and it works well with the new power you are developing right now.

But don't stick with my mantra if you can come up with something that's better for you. Feel free to choose anything that makes you feel like a warrior.

When you change the way that you talk to yourself, you change the way that you think. And the more you change the way you think, the more you will be able to stay positive.

No matter who you talk to, adopt and consistently practice a new way of being about what you're thinking at all times. And, stay positive.

When your brain is in a positive emotional state, you carry that state with you wherever you go. The more that you practice 'fun' and joy, the more you will feel like life is fun and joyful.

Here's a practice you can use to make your power your best accessory.

- Close your eyes and think of a time when you were really powerful.

- Stop and visualize what was happening, what the environment was like, who was there, how you felt, etc.

- Bring yourself back into that feeling and into that emotional state.

- When you are ready, open your eyes and write or talk about what you saw.

- Listen to yourself to see if you are focusing on what you saw, what you heard, or what you felt.

- When you listen to the way you describe the state you were in, you will probably notice that you focused on sights, sounds, or feelings.

- No matter what you focused on, there are ways to bring yourself back to this good feeling.

- SIGHT: If you focused on sights, think about a picture you can carry with you that will remind you of the powerful state you were in. When you need to feel powerful, look at the picture or envision it in your mind until you feel that power again.

- SOUND: If you focused on sounds, then think about a song or a sound that might remind you of when you felt powerful. Make sure you can always listen to the sound when you're in a situation where you might not feel as powerful.

- FEELING: When you focus on the feelings of a situation, you will have to find something that will bring you back to those sensations. For example, if you touched something cold, then you need to be able to feel something cold when you're not feeling as powerful.

This practice is called anchoring, which is a fancy term for remembering what you felt in the past and using it to feel the same way now.

A practice of NLP (neuro-linguistic programming) is to retrain your brain to be more positive and productive.

When you tap into past emotions, you can tap into emotions you want to have now.

Pretty cool, right?

You don't need to get out a textbook to use this either. All you have to do is re-direct your thoughts, or tell them to stop, whenever you start thinking something you shouldn't be.

Stop yourself and think back to a good time. When you anchor back into this good time, you will feel more powerful. You will create a positive thought instead of a negative one.

You are training yourself to be better to yourself.

And you can do it on your own – no therapist necessary.

Once you have enjoyed this series of mental spa treatments, you will find you are more rejuvenated and better prepared to handle negative situations around you.

You will realize that what happens around you is out of your control, but the way you feel about what happens to you is in your control.

You have the power. You always have.

When you rediscover your power, your experience of yourself and your style will be positive – no matter what anyone says.

In fact, you might not hear the criticism anymore because you sincerely believe it does not apply to you.

And it doesn't. It never did.

Talk Yourself Up

Sometimes, you just have to shout in order to be heard. So, why are we so afraid of speaking up for ourselves?

We might be the first one to scream FIRE, but when it comes to talking about the beautiful creatures we are, why do we go mute?

You look great and everyone around you should know it.

Now, this is not about becoming a conceited person, or living your life as if the world exists only to serve you. Not at all.

But what you are going to learn right now are the best ways to promote the amazing person you are, so that you can remind yourself just how amazing you are.

- **Talk about accomplishments:** Tell others what you have done since they may have no idea all that you do and all that you're capable of doing. Mention the incredible things you have done and they will ask you for more details.

- **Be ready to tell your own story:** When you're listening to a conversation and you have something to offer, speak up. Tell your story, and what you have experienced. Your opinions should be heard too.

- **Don't downplay your accomplishments:** Actually, it's common for us to downplay what we've achieved in life. *Oh yeah, I got the promotion, but it's really no big deal...* Your accomplishments do matter and they should never be downplayed.

While you don't want to be a braggart, you also shouldn't be invisible. When you have something to say:

- Tell a few close friends.
- Tell your family.
- Tell your pets.
- Tell your co-workers.
- Tell a stranger.

Everyone deserves to hear just how great you are and what you contribute to the world.

When you're sharing, here are some tips to make sure you don't venture into annoying-ville.

- **State the facts:** When you're gushing about yourself, you might want to focus on the facts. When you're exaggerating, people can sense it, and they will think you're full of bull the next time you have something to say.

- **Ask what they have accomplished:** Make sure to focus immediately on the other person after you've shared something exciting. And be genuinely interested in what they have to say. This is going to make you a better person in the end.

- **Keep it short:** When you want to talk about how amazing you are, don't go on and on. Keep what you have to say short and the other person will have a chance to listen and absorb your message. They will hear the information, react accordingly, and wait their turn to talk about themselves.

- **Don't hide your passion:** If you're really excited about what's happened, don't hide it. Passion is infectious.

When you're ready to talk about yourself, others will be ready to listen.

You are a person with things to share and things to express, and with the style you've created, you'll be all the more confident in who you are, what you look like, and what you have to give to the world.

You're probably feeling really good about yourself right now.

I'm glad, because you should.

Confident All the Time

Confidence, while it looks like something people are born with, is actually a state of mind that takes time to develop and sustain.

Though there may be days when you're more confident than others, you can create a state of mind that keeps you confident 98% of the time.

That means you're going to be ready for anything.

You can keep your confidence in tact by:

- Listing your accomplishments.
- Creating goals.
- Reaching goals.
- Associating yourself with confident folks.

Every month, write out a list of all of the things you did that were wonderful and positive.

Even listing the things that no one else will ever know – like the month where you actually kept the bathroom clean, or the day when you took down the holiday decorations – will help you feel more confident.

Think of the fact that when you notice these things, you fill your brain with positive accomplishments and energy.

And the more you fill your brain with great stuff, the less room there is for anything that isn't positive or productive.

While this sounds like more work, creating new goals and reaching those goals is a super way to make sure you're confident all of the time.

When you make a goal, you make a promise to yourself that you will reach a certain milestone by a certain period of time. It's something you plan for, organize for, and then execute.

With each goal you successfully reach, you will be more confident that you can reach the next goal. And the next one.

Pretty soon, you will believe that no matter what you want to do, you can do it. And you will do it.

Each week, try to set a few goals for yourself. Whether they're related to style or not, isn't important.

What is important is that you focus on coming up with things that you want to do, make a plan to do them, and then do them.

Make a list of goals and watch how great you feel when you cross things off. The more you cross off, the more you have done, the more productive you have been, and the more energy you have to do more.

You can set style goals for yourself each week – or promises to read certain sections of this book. And then do it.

When you do, you are getting things done – and you are creating self-confidence that can't be stopped.

You've heard it before, but you should hear it again: associate yourself with confident folks.

You want to ditch the people in your life who are always complaining about how horrible everything is.

They're just not worth your time, or your energy.

You should be with people who are and who want to be more amazing than they are right now. Be with people who are positive about their lives and who want to make sure they are getting everything they want from life.

The more you are around them, the more you will learn about how to be confident in yourself, and the more you will learn about how being confident feels.

Infectious power comes from being with powerful people. Don't waste your time with anyone else.

The practices you have learned in this chapter should be done regularly so that they can make the most impact on your goals!

Compliment Yourself NOW

Right now, get out a piece of paper and write down all of the words that describe yourself. For example, here's a list you can start with.

Circle the ones that you like.

- Beautiful
- Gorgeous
- Amazing
- Sexy
- Stunning
- _____ (Write in any word of your choice.)

When you compliment yourself, you're telling your brain that you are what you say you are.

What you might not realize is that every thought you give to your brain is a thought it believes.

Though you might not believe all of the compliments at first, your brain does. Your brain will hold onto these thoughts like a life raft, keeping them close and coming back to them when it needs a boost.

Program your thoughts, and your thoughts become your life.

And the more compliments you 'feed' your brain, the more hungry it will become. It will begin to crave those compliments, not the other things you used to tell yourself.

You look gorgeous, dammit. Get used to it!

4

The Honest Truth Is All That Matters

Truth is something that we want to tell ourselves, but we may be afraid of what it will mean.

We want the truth from everyone else in our lives. We want to know that others like us.

We want to believe that others love us.

But when it comes to ourselves, we seem more willing to settle for less. We are willing to say that everything we want to believe is just lies.

> We can't be beautiful.
> We can't be stylish.
> We can't be the someone who turns heads.

But what if you can?

When you start being honest with yourself, you realize things are different. You realize that YOU are different.

As you look in the mirror and tell yourself the truth, that you are powerful, that you can change what you want to change, that you can BE whomever you want to be, that's when you will surprise yourself.

If you can't believe what you say to yourself, who can you believe?

You CAN Handle the Truth

The truth is more than just the things that you WANT to believe. At first, it might seem that way. But the things you tell yourself about how fabulous you are are truths. Those are things you should have been telling yourself all along.

No matter what clothes you put on, you are still all of the things you tell yourself.

You can tell yourself the truth about your power. You can handle it.

What you should do right now is:

- Stop lying to yourself.
- Remind yourself of all that you are.
- Be open to changing what you don't like.

Right now, you are stronger than ever before. Even if you notice that something isn't working for you, you can handle it.

You can make sure that you are better for knowing what you know and then moving into something new.

You CAN do it.

If you're not sure you're telling yourself the truth, ask these questions:

- Is this true for me?
- Would someone else say this to me?

- Would my friend say this to me?
- Would I say this to a friend?

We can be brutally honest with our friends, but it's challenging to offer that same service to ourselves.

If you want to build a lifelong relationship with yourself, start 'fessing up.

Create a new way of looking at yourself, a new way of looking at what you tell yourself.

Am I telling myself the truth? Am I following my truth?

Perhaps you're not sure if you can handle the truth if it's not too pretty.

Sure, you can tell yourself you're amazing, but if you're not the weight you want to be, or you're not taking care of yourself, then can you really say that you're as powerful or as beautiful as you think you are?

Yes you can!

Just because you might want to change a few things doesn't make you any less of a person.

It doesn't make you a person without value.

Instead, change the way that you approach the hard truth.

You can change if that's what will make you happy.

Think about the things that are hard truths about yourself and consider what you can do about it.

Boldly stand up to your truth, ask what it wants, and tell it what you will do.

> Be bold.
> Be courageous.
> Be powerful.

You are worth all of these actions – and more.

Your style is just one of your weapons to authentically represent your truth to the world. When you represent your truth, you have nothing to hide.

You are yourself, which is who you want to be.

And while you may have moments where it seems easier to lie, think about how it feels to not have to be anything less than who you are.

The process begins with you.

Change begins with you.

And you know what? When you're the one who's in control of your truth and your power, you're the one that can stand up and say, YES, I DID IT.

Yes you did.

How To Keep Your Style, How To Keep Your Power

Now that you're all supercharged with style, power and truth, hold onto it.

You have all the tools you need, but sometimes, you're going to have moments when things won't seem as easy as they once did at first.

Think about a diet you tried.

The first few days, even the first week, you were excited about what you were doing and you followed the diet without a second thought.

You could do everything on your eating plan; you made it to the gym, and you felt GREAT.

Then life jumped in.

You stood on the scale and found that the number was higher than you thought it should be. Someone told you that your diet wasn't the right one.

Someone laughed at your workout regimen.

You thought to yourself, *what's the use?*

You went back to the old ways you were eating and exercising. And things didn't change...all because other people in your life were telling you that you were wrong.

Or you maybe have tried to quit smoking; then something horrible happened in your life, so you started smoking again.

These old ways are crutches. They're so easy to fall back on.

Habits are hard to break – but they can certainly be broken. Instead of living off of the energy you've built up with this book, prepare yourself and your mind for the times when things will get sticky again.

What happens when life doesn't seem to agree with what you're doing?

- **Remind yourself of your goals:** When you feel like things are making you feel less than fabulous, remind yourself of what you want to achieve. It will get you back on track.

- **Talk to positive folks:** Stop hanging out with the naysayers. Stick with the people who make you feel good about yourself and your life, without 'telling you what you want to hear'.

- **Wear something beautiful:** Of course, putting on your favorite outfit will also help you feel pretty darn fantastic.

- **Stick to your plan:** No matter what anyone else says, stick to the plan in this book. Think about what you're doing and DO IT.

- **Remember how far you've come:** You've already changed so much and found yourself to be quite an incredible person, but sometimes you have to remind yourself of where you've been, to know just how far you've come.

The world isn't always going to be easy on you.

But you can only change what *you* think, not necessarily what *they* think. By prepping now for that 'style emergency,' you will be ready for anything or anyone.

No one should be able to take away your sunshine or your power ever again.

Keep it right where you want it.

The Danger of Little White Lies

The lies that you tell others aren't helping you, and the little white lies that you tell yourself aren't going to do you any good.

First of all, they breed.

When you tell one lie, you have to tell another lie to cover it up, and before you know it, you've covered yourself with a mess of problematic lies.

Little white lies are not the answer.

Sure, they make you feel good, in that moment, but what about the long term?

Lying to yourself and to others can:

- **Become a habit:** When you lie once, you realize how easy it is to do. And then you do it again and again and again...

- **Make you unsure of the truth:** Lies subtly make you think that anything you hear isn't the truth. Doubting yourself and others around you isn't very stylish.

- **Cause you to question yourself:** When you lie, you question yourself, and your integrity. It's not worth it.

- **Cause you to question others:** Even more concerning is that when you lie, you question others. Who has time for that?

While you may never have thought style could be connected to the idea of lying, it is.

When you want to have power, when you want to reclaim your power, you need to reclaim the truth too.

Think of it as a fashion accessory that always goes with your outfit. And it's always a trend that you can wear confidently.

Forget the lies. They never helped you anyway.

They're sort of like having too much plastic surgery. They might hide the problem, but they're not going to work forever.

You'll have to keep going back for more. And you deserve better!

A New and Powerful You

Welcome to you. The new and powerful you. This is the you that you always knew was inside. You just weren't sure how to unleash her.

When you coaxed her out with pretty clothes and compliments, she ran out into the world. And she's ready for more than just a new pair of shoes.

She's ready to take on bigger and better things.

You're ready to do all of the things that you want to do:

- Find love.
- Get that promotion.
- Tell your friends the truth.
- Be successful at home.
- Create the life you always dreamt of while dressing your best!

When you are powerful, SHOW UP and take charge of your life!

You're playing the game of life – and you're winning it.

Reward yourself for all the work you've done.

- **Find an accessory to wear:** Sometimes, it's fun to find one accessory that reminds you of all the hard work you've done to find your power again. Wear it as a sentimental reminder whenever you need a boost.

- **Take yourself out:** Why not treat yourself by going out to dinner tonight?

- **Pamper your body:** Head to the spa and allow your body to feel as beautiful as you are. Allow yourself to be cared for and celebrated.

You deserve all this and more.

5

A Bolder New YOU

Once upon a time, you thought that being stylish and dressing your best was simply about wearing a certain color in one season and another color in another season.

Maybe you thought that having the right shoes or the right accessories would make you happy.

But time and time again, they didn't.

In this book, you've learned the true secrets of style, but also the secrets of power. When you look at style as a way to tap into your power, the power that makes you uniquely amazing, you will ALWAYS look good.

I promise.

Stephany's Seven Style Secrets

You've gotten this far and you've learned so much, not only about your closet, but also about yourself.

You've learned my style secrets.

1. Love Yourself No Matter What
2. Flatter Your Figure, Forget Your Flaws
3. Dress For Yourself, Not Anyone Else
4. Life Without a Mirror
5. Discover Your Personal Style
6. Risks Equal Rewards
7. You Look Great, Dammit!

And while these might not seem conventional, they're certainly going to help you get the most out of your life – no matter what.

These secrets aren't about trying to make you look a certain way. I'm not going to tell you what you should or should not wear.

I want you to find the style and the power that was inside you all along.

Use your style to access your power and you will have the power to be the person you want to be and do anything you want to do.

And grab hold of everything you want in life.

Where DO You Go From Here?

What can you do with all of this power? What can you do with all of this knowledge?

I have a few ideas.

First of all, you can go out into the world a little less fearful than you were before. You can take chances, take risks, and start to understand that you are the one who calls the shots in your own life.

No one else.

You can try out new styles and new ways to express yourself.

You can talk to people you would have never talked to before.

You can launch a new venture that you were too afraid to start.

You can enjoy your life and everything you do in it.

But what's even more important?

You can inspire others!

When people want to know what makes you so fabulous – let them know they are fabulous.

When others want to know what your secret is – let them know that you know seven secrets.

Spread the word that you are powerful, strong, and authentically stylish.

You are worth the changes you've made to your life because they make you happy. And YOU deserve to be happy. Right now.

Is There A Limit To Your Power?

The only limit to your power is YOU.

Never impose limits on how much you can get out of life.

> You can do anything you want to do.
> You have to believe it.

So put on your best dress.

Start styling your new life.

And...

Be happy to be YOU!

About the Author

Stephany Greene, also known as the 'First Lady of Style', is a sought after Celebrity Style Expert, Educator, Life Stylist, Fashion Designer, TV Producer, TV Host and Fashion Show Producer. With her book, *Stephany's Style Secrets - 7 Steps to Live and Dress Your Best,* Stephany shares her more than 20 years of fashion industry expertise where her collections as a Fashion Designer and Design Director garnered $75 million for Calvin Klein, Tommy Hilfiger, Ralph Lauren, Perry Ellis, The NBA and The NFL, among others. *Stephany's Style Secrets* highlights her signature technique of using her own down-to-earth personality to offer expert style advice, which has impacted everyone from aspiring fashion students, to nationally recognized celebrities, athletes and politicians.

Considered a respected authority on the business and politics of fashion, as President of Stephany & Company, LLC, she is changing the landscape of the industry, by spearheading the fashion education movement in the nation's capitol. Stephany made history when she founded the first Fashion Merchandising Program at the University of the District of Columbia (CC). Her program attracted 'Skills for America's Future,' a White House Initiative announced by President Obama, as one of seven college programs in the U.S. chosen for a partnership by $14 billion retail giant, Gap, Inc., for career training and scholarships. As the lead professor, Stephany also taught the fifteen fashion courses she developed for the college.

Stephany's personal voice and style has been celebrated in her self-branded *The Politics of Style* ™ blog, as featured on *Essence Magazine's* website, *Essence.com,* with over 90,000 visitors. She executive produces major fashion shows, including events she co-hosts for Bloomingdale's department store and *Essence Magazine.* Stephany has served as a keynote speaker for the Executive Office of the Mayor of Washington, D.C. and the National Museum for Women in the Arts.

A native Washingtonian, Stephany is featured in the premiere coffee table book, the *Inaugural Edition of The Best of D.C.,* and she has appeared in national media, on television and radio, including *Details Magazine, Essence Magazine, Washington Life Magazine, The Baltimore Sun*, Fox News, New Jersey News 12, WPGC 95.5FM, and WHUR 96.3FM.

Stephany earned a Masters Degree from American University in Public Communication and a Bachelor of Fine Arts Degree in Fashion Design from Pratt Institute. She also studied Fashion Design at Parsons School of Design in Paris, France. In 1999, Stephany's alma mater, Pratt Institute, established the '*Stephany Greene Sportswear Award*' in her honor, as a recognized addition to its Annual Fashion Show.

Visit Stephany's websites: www.stephanygreene.com
                               www.stephanysstylesecrets.com

Media and personal appearances: management@stephanygreene.com